LIVING LIFE
IN RUBY SLIPPERS

A woman's healing journey from diagnosis of
Brain Tumour to Wellness

KATHLEEN HARRISON

Contents

Part two

"Follow the Yellow Brick Road"

Acknowledgements

To my husband John, for your support, with lots of love

My daughters Stefanie and Claire, and son David - for picking me to be your mother, even if we have been through a difficult time.

To my sister, brothers and sister-in-law, who gave their support during these trying times.

My friends Kate and Marjorie, who were at the end of the phone when I needed a chat, or who took the time to visit me.

Dr. Deepika Rodrigo, Ayurveda Doctor, for her Skype consultations, oils and herbs.

Liz Weir and all at Northumbria Healers, my spiritual family, who gave me peace and tranquillity.

Mandy Moseley, Shiatsu, who was generous with treatments and love.

Glynis Rose, for her Ayurvedic massages and Yoga practice.

Pat McBride, from The Pituitary Foundation who supported me during this storytelling.

Martin Crosby, who was responsible for setting up a Pituitary Support Group in Newcastle upon Tyne. This is where I met and talked to others with the same condition or similar.

Dawn and Holly who helped me with my rehabilitation and recovery of my sense of fun.

To all of the team at Sight Service - just for being there at this time in my life.

Sue White, who drove me to lunches with the Horsley Writing Group. This is where I was given inspiration in my writing.

My daughter Claire, and my niece Vicky, who took the time to proofread and edit this story.

Thank you to all.

Part One
"From the far north they heard a low wail of the wind"

Chapter One

1 "I shall take the heart, for the brains do not make one happy, and happiness is the best"

"I wish we knew whether it was a boy or a girl" I said to John as we browsed the baby clothes. Not too long now, until both of us are off to Australia. In November we fly to see our daughter Claire and her husband Tony who live in Melbourne. After 6 years of trying for a baby and on the second attempt at IVF, the baby is due in December and we, my husband John and I, were going to be there and stay with them for 8 weeks over the Christmas and into New Year.

It was October and I needed some new glasses, and of course sun glasses, because it would be summer in November when we landed at Melbourne Airport.

"There is a problem with your field vision" said the optician in Boots, "I want you to go to the eye hospital and have it checked out. I will write a letter for you to take. Come back in an hour. I will have it ready for you". I was in the shop anyway so I looked at more baby stuff, so excited for a new grandchild, our miracle baby.

The following day we went to the Royal Victoria Infirmary's Eye Department as an emergency case. I was examined by the ophthalmologist and was tested on various machines. "There is a growth on your pituitary gland" said the ophthalmologist "but they have wonderful medicines these days." She continued, "Oh and the endocrinologist is going to be passing the department and he will pop in and chat to you".

The Doctor sat opposite John and me. He explained the situation as kindly as he could.

"It's a straight forward operation" said the endocrinologist

"The Neurosurgeons do this on a daily basis; you will be in hospital for a couple of days with a week's recovery at home".

I looked at John, he was grey.

"How do you feel?" said the doctor, "now I have explained. Maybe a bit better?" He continued "On a scale of 0 – 10, how do you feel now?" I looked hard at this man. I said "Shit! We are going to Australia on 21 November; can it wait till we get back? Our daughter is going to have her first baby and she wants us to be there."

"Let's have a scan and see what's what first" he responded. "These tumours are 99% benign so it will be fine. You will be OK" he said getting up and gesturing for us to follow. "Come on let's get some blood out of you."

We were numb. Our world was being turned upside down. We sat for a while in the hospital café drinking tea and coffee. It was OK for the doctor to say no problem, you will be fine. Our feelings were racing because, over the last three years and even before, two brothers-in-law had passed away with a brain tumour also John's mum was diagnosed with a brain tumour and other forms of cancer. Three years previous John was diagnosed with bowel cancer and went through an emergency operation. He was on the operating table for more than 6 hours on the Friday and had to go through another operation the following Wednesday because there was a problem from the first operation. So what did the doctor know?

John was a National Health Service baby being one of the first to be born in a hospital. Whereas I was born the year before that, 1947, one of 7 babies delivered by my Aunty. My Mam and Dad used the old fashion medicines to treat illness - herbs, lotions and potions. We never went to see the Doctor in those days either. I was from a different generation. The National Health Service (NHS) didn't hold much sway for me. I had continued all of my life, and with my children, using herbal and homeopathic and other complementary ways to stay well or heal so it was a big shock to find something was amiss. Having said that my reflexology friend told me the previous year, and this year, there was a problem with my eyes. That is why I visited the opticians. A tumour was pressing on the optic nerve and that was causing the field vision loss. I had felt there was a problem. I would flick my hair out of my eyes - thought my fringe was in the way - strange I would think, I didn't have a fringe.

We sat until the numbness and shock wore off. "Let's go Christmas shopping; we are in the city so we can shop for presents for Tyler." Tyler was our only grandchild at that time; he would be 5½ by Christmas. Feeling a little bit better at the prospect, because we were going to Australia, off we went.

The letter arrived from the Royal Victoria Infirmary (R.V.I) giving us the scan appointment – November 5 at 6.30pm – our wedding anniversary – 42 years married. What a way to celebrate!!

We had told our children who lived in Newcastle upon Tyne what was what. Stefanie was the eldest (Tyler's mum) and she was married to Jamie. David was the youngest, and he was married to Laura. We didn't tell Claire as we were worried because she was pregnant. We didn't want to upset her at this point; we wanted to tell her face to face.

On the day of the scan, David and Laura said

"Why don't we go to a Tapas bar on the Quayside in Newcastle before the scan?" (They were giving us a lift to the hospital) "And it can at least be a small celebration for you both". We agreed a good idea

"Well, it will take the edge off it all" I said.

The tapas bar was a good diversion. It would take my mind of it all for a bit. I felt better as we sat there, John and me, with our son and daughter –in-law. The bar was large and empty, not another person at any of the tables but then it was tea time everyone would still be at work finishing off their day. It was cold in there so we kept our coats on. The waiter popped back and forwards reassuring us,

"It will warm up. The engineer is sorting it out" he continued, "It's the central heating. Sorry!", then off he went. It was a bit like a Fawlty Towers episode.

When the waiter came to take our orders "Can we have a discount?" my daughter in law said. We all laughed, she hated being taken for a ride.

Chapter Two

2 "There is a cyclone on the way" said Uncle Henry"

I was alone at home when the mail arrived. Three letters all marked NHS on the envelopes.

I opened the first:

Would you please attend Royal Victoria Infirmary on November 26 at 7:00 for your operation?

They are having a laugh, I thought, they know I'm off to Australia on the 21st. I will not be here.

I opened the second one.

Would you please attend a pre - op clinic on Monday 13 November? Stupid people .....

I opened the third letter.

Your appointment at the endocrine department is 20 November at 10:30.

It slowly dawned on me we were not going to Australia...... John would be back soon and we would have to, at some point in the next few hours, tell Claire and Tony we would not be there with them during their very special time. We had not mentioned what was going on with me, because we did not want to burst their bubble and they were 12000 miles away. Anyway we would talk about it face to face when we got there but now......

We Skyped the next morning, it was their evening. "Hi" they said cheerfully.

"We've got tickets for a carol service in the Botanic Gardens in Melbourne on Christmas Eve". "Oh" continued Claire "we are going on the restaurant tram for lunch for your wedding anniversary, and ours on Dec 1. You're crying, Mum?"

"Yes" I said.

"We cannot come over there, I am not well, and I have to have an operation on 26 November".

"Why?" said Tony.

I could see Claire was very upset by this time.

"I've got a tumour on my pituitary gland, I am so sorry I have spoilt everything." I believed that this condition was of my own making because life is what you make of it. It is created from our own consciousness. Any illness or condition is created by the negative thoughts so it was for me to find out what I had been thinking which had created this condition.

"So very, very, sorry darlings."

"You will be fine" said Tony "We are very disappointed you cannot come but you have to sort yourself first Kath."

The following day we parcelled up the new baby clothes, blankets, little things we had bought to take to Australia when we flew out there. We had also Christmas presents for the baby and we planned to buy presents for Claire and Tony and for ourselves when we got there. The result of all this joyful shopping was two boxes, one of which we titled "Baby Box" and the other "Christmas Box". We went to the local post office to send them. The postmaster said jokingly "It might be cheaper to take these yourself, that's £150 please….."

"We wish", we both said together.

Chapter Three

3 "It was Toto that made Dorothy laugh"

November 26 2013

"Think of something really nice to take you under as I give you the anaesthetic" the anaesthetist said. The day had arrived: November 26. I am sitting in the pre-op room with John beside me.

"That's easy; it's been Christmas morning in our house this morning" and I explained that "because we had to be at the hospital by 7.00 am so we were up at about 5am". A Skype signal alerted us that Claire was on line from Australia.

"Hi Mam the packages have arrived, thank you so much".

Tony was like a kid in a toy shop looking at the goodies from the "Baby Box". He had a baby hat on his head, and was holding up the sign, heart shaped, that read "Baby in the House". In his other hand was the oblong box which we had sent; it was to hold the birth certificate.

"We love it all" said Claire. "The "Christmas Box" is under the tree, look, it's ready to open with you at Christmas". She continued "Remember your Christmas Eve, our Christmas morning"

"All the best", Claire said, "You will be fine".

"All the best to you two too, keep us up to date as best you can" said John, because I was in tears.

"Goodbye, my lovelies".

"Love you forever".

And so it was my early Christmas morning on 26 November that was the last thought I had as I went under.

Chapter Four

4 "I am anxious to get back to my aunt and uncle I am sure they will worry about me"

John's Story

November 26 2013

Brian, a good friend from work, had offered to pick us up and take us to the hospital. "Save you the hassle of parking" he said. He dropped us off just after 7:00 am.
Kath and I walked to the ward and registered. We tried to chat but both of us were worried. The nurses were very kind. The anaesthetist came and explained what would happen. It all went over so quickly, then the nurse said "OK Kathleen, time to go. Phone us about lunchtime, John, she should be back by then".

I walked to work, only about a mile but my longest walk ever. I didn't want to leave Kath.

In the office I tried to concentrate on my job as the Finance Director, but people kept coming in and asking how things were: John the MD who had known Kath since 1996, Brian, a really good friend, and also the Training Manager for the company, the training staff, even the hairdressers in the shop downstairs.

1:00 pm
"Any news from the hospital yet?" Brian said. "No nothing yet" I replied. "I think I will ring, they said about lunch time and its 1 o'clock now so hopefully it's all done and dusted." I was trying to sound cheerful but wasn't really. "No, she isn't back yet. Ring again in an hour." You wonder why the extra time and your mind races.

2:00pm
I phone again. Still not back. Why is a 3 hour operation taking so long? "You could phone again in an hour."

3:00pm
Same story. Panic sets in.

4:00pm
"We expect her back within the hour. We will call you."

Brian comes in. I tell him the story. "Come on, I'm driving you up there now."

Brian drops me off. "Call if you need anything, a lift or whatever" he says.

5:00pm
I'm sitting in Costa Coffee in the hospital, having a latte but not tasting it. I phone again. "She is in Recovery. Come up and we'll come for you when she is settled. Ward 18".

I get to Ward 18, a notice outside reads "High Dependency Unit".

I sit and sit and sit. Lots of people like me, waiting for news. We all shuffle and mutter but largely it's just a deafening silence. People get called, but not me.

6:30pm

"Mr Harrison? You can come through now."

I follow the nurse in silence. I want to ask so many questions but the words stick in my throat. I go through so many doors. I cleanse my hands. The nurse leads me to the far corner. A young nurse says "Hello, I'm Steffi. I'm looking after Kath". Kath is on a high bed, connected to all sorts of machines, her head swathed in bandages, and a patch covering her right eye. She doesn't stir. "What happened?" I ask.

"It was much more difficult than they thought. She has been through a lot"

"Is she OK?"

"We will keep her here for about 24 hours then see how she is".

I sat and held Kath's hand, and spoke softly to her, not knowing if she could hear me. What did I say? I have no idea!! I just wanted her to know I was there.

I needed to tell our children, but I didn't want to leave her. Finally, I asked about phoning and I was shown into a side room where I phoned, first Stefanie, then David. Stefanie had her little boy Tyler who was 5 years old. I told her Mum was ok, but very tired and not to come in until tomorrow. David said he would come in and take me home. He came in with Laura, his wife, and by that time Kath was awake but only just. We chatted for a little bit, and then they took me home.

They asked if I wanted to stay with them but I said no, I'll stay at home. When I got in there were so many messages on the home phone and texts on the mobile, I didn't know where to start. I just sat down and cried my eyes out.

Chapter Five

5 "It wasn't Australia or even OZ"

November 28 2013

"Come on Kath, wake up. I'm Steffi."

I opened my eyes I wasn't in Australia, never mind OZ after a bump on my head. Beside my bed were my Stefanie and John. It was the nurse who was called Steffi, same name as my daughter. "Thank you God" I quietly thought "you sent me an angel with the same name as my daughter".

"Are you ok?" she said. "Yes, is the operation over?" I asked.

"Yes it is, and you are now in the High Dependency Ward, been here for a couple of days but they hope to put you on a proper bed this afternoon". John interjected "No baby yet" he said.

"I know because I am still here" I replied thinking; I had not died on the operating table. Even though I knew it was very rare for that to happen.

We were told this when John went for his second operation to repair the bowel following the operation to remove the bowel cancer. It was the anaesthetist at the time who told us. The anaesthetist had said that it's generally after the op.... whether or not people had the strength and courage to get over it. So the next few days would show whether or not I had courage and strength. I also knew the next few days would be strange. I don't know why but it was in my head that I would die to give spirit to this new life. The baby was due at the beginning of December but Claire seemed to think it would come early. It was now 28 November, "the stage was set".

November 29

Usually doctors etc. did their morning rounds each day. This morning it was a visit from the surgeon and sidekicks who performed the operation. There were two things I wanted to know.

"Did you get it all out?" I asked.

At the pre-operation interview I was told that if it didn't all come out during the operation I would have to have another operation, and before Christmas, so wanted to know.

"Did you get it all out?"

"Yes" replied the surgeon, so no further operation needed"

The second thing I wanted to know was…

"Did I have a stroke during the op?"

The left side of my body had no feeling….paralysed.

"No" replied the surgeon.

Chapter Six

6 "They were not as big as the grown folk she had always been used
to"

December 4 2013

Here we are again, another night over. Slept well, a bit fitful but from
8p.m. the previous evening till 6.30 a.m. today

John always came on the ward around 11 o' clock. When he arrived, he got
out his Galaxy tablet, and set up a Skype call to Claire as I lay in bed.

"Claire texted me this morning" he said. "She said to Skype when I got to the
hospital" he was on line and so was Claire. Her voice came through.

"Hello Mam and Dad, I got something to show you, say hello to your new
grandson." It was a boy. Oh joy of joys the baby was born. We didn't know
what the gender of the baby was going to be, Claire and Tony did not want to
know. This pregnancy had been the second attempt at IVF and that was
enough for them, they were going to have a baby. This was one of the
reasons we wanted to be with them…. a miracle baby.

I began to cry with joy. Not only at the arrival of the baby but I was still alive.
Melbourne was 11 hours ahead of us in time. The baby was born at 5.37 pm
on 4 December in Australia. In England it would have been 6.37 a.m. in the
morning of 4 December and I had lived through it. I was still alive.

Claire's voice broke through my thoughts. "I never did get the chance to tell
you Mam, this baby is a rainbow baby, its soul is brand new, he never been on
earth before." An ah ha moment. I thought, "That's why I am still here".
Rainbow children are new souls that have never been to earth before. He
didn't need my old soul. I remembered where the thought came from. When
I was a child my mother used to say "hatch, match, and dispatch". When a
baby is born someone has to die to make way for the new child or spirit.
Whether true or false who knows? I was still here.

Chapter Severn

7 "Truth is within you, do not search for it elsewhere" – Osho

December 11 2013

One of the things I always did in my life was writing in a diary, which I called Morning Pages. These pages were the idea of an author called Julia Cameron in her book "The Artist's Way". She believed that writing every morning, on getting up, before breakfast, or getting ready, brought up all sorts of issues that might be lurking in our subconscious. This practice is often called "a stream of consciousness".

I continued to do this writing when I was in hospital, almost every day during the weeks I was there. I continued for more than that during a year's recovery at home. This Novel is the result of doing that.

The following part of this Chapter is the beginning of writing after the surgery which readers, is why it's rather weird but I felt I had to represent it a little bit as written in the Diary. So as Miranda Hart would say in her show "Bear with, bear with".

Well pages nice to be together again. I wrote in an A4 writing pad. Cleaner be in soon.

Joyce, the domestic, came into the room every day. She does a fabulous job. The room is light and fresh, airy, it's got a lovely smell, and it's a credit to her. It seems this ward won awards for cleanliness, so good on her.

The room is the usual clinical hospital room. It is square with beige tiled floor. The walls are painted a pale soft sky blue. On the left of my bed there is a brown door into and out of the room. Beside the door is a window that looks onto the actual ward. Oh, the bed has a plastic mattress. This kind of mattress is used to help stop bed sores. The bedding is a sheet to lie on. An over sheet and a green cellular blanket, you know the usual hospital bedding. There is a big window with horizontal blinds looking out onto the world. The ward is on fifth floor. I can see the sky. To my right beside the big window there is another door which goes to the en-suite. This room contains a walk in shower, a sink and a toilet. The walls in this room are white and there are hand rails around attached with easy access from each receptacle.

There is a blue leather straight backed chair beside my clinical bed. I move between bed and chair. This was my world. Still breathing. All is well. I remembered when I awoke for the first time in this room by myself, I thought "Own room? I must be going to die" because I thought a patient only got their own room if they were going to die. They knew it. I thought I would die at that time. Baby was born now and I was still alive so really had to give myself a chance now to get over the surgery. I was going to be in hospital a lot longer than the 3 to 4 days with a week to recover at home. They told me this in the beginning, laughing out loud. What a laugh!!

I would write all sorts of rubbish. The brain needed a rest, after what it and my head had been through. The surgeons had to go into the side of my head to get access to the tumour sitting on the pituitary gland. Usually the procedure is to go up the nose because the pituitary gland is at the back of the head behind the nose. It was not possible to do this for me, the tumour was bigger. The surgeon said on the pre-operation visit "the tumour was going around the corners" therefore they decided going in the side of the head was to be the best option. Any kind of head injury from a little bump, as we know, even leaves the head and brain traumatised. There was a drain pipe sticking out of my head. During and after any surgery there is a pipe going to the site of the operation. This pipe takes away any fluid from the wound site. After a few days the charge nurse came into my room.
"Hello Kath, shall we take out the pipe?" he said.
"Will it hurt?" I asked, terrified.
"No" said the nurse.
I braced myself.
"All done" he said.
"You have done it? I didn't feel a thing, Thank you" I said almost in tears. All of this head activity and no pain.
My writing was strange, couldn't remember how to spell words and that's if I could remember what the words were I was searching for. Below is an example. Looking back at it, I didn't know what I was trying to say.

Sitting in the chair now, not some time here is good to Nearly ? Think nice things cold milk.

I think the above was about sitting in the chair, by my bed. At this time I was using only my left eye to see what was written. The right eye was closed. It's the left eye that had the vision that at this stage even if it was hazy. The doctor said I only had central vision in it. I had loss of peripheral vision. As they say, in the land of the blind the one eyed man is king. There were a lot of question marks in all of my writing during the early days. I found that strange because John said my stitches and the resulting scar were like a reverse question mark in shape. Mm I thought, and there were a lot of questions needing answers?

Wonder how my Claire and Bude are? Hope they had a good day. Managed to peel a segment of Satsuma?? With the right hand. The other hand and left side of body have no feeling in it since the surgery.

My concern about my daughter and her baby in Australia… how were they managing? I should have been there to help out. Of course they did manage. The other rambling…. I was thrilled at managing to peel a Satsuma that had been left for me. I placed it on the table over my bed. It had a sticky mat on it, to hold items in place. Lucky for me the Satsuma was good and stayed still as I peeled it, using only my right hand and finger nails..

"Have I had a stroke?" I asked the surgeon and her sidekicks when they visited the next day.
 "No" said the chief surgeon.
There was three of them, speak no evil, see no evil, and hear no evil. It was days later by accident I found out what had happened.
 "Did you have a stroke?" said the nurse, as she came into my room and pottered around. She continued
"Oh no you didn't, it was a bleed during the operation".

"Thank you, that explains the left side of my body being paralysed" I responded.

Now and? Level the? Is the thought of through

 The above was about my salt levels.
It was the doctor's round. "Your salt levels are not good" was this morning's joy.
"I do not do salt" I replied.
"It's because of the operation" the doctor replied.
"The way to rectify this problem is for you to drink less" He continued.
"You can only drink 500 mils a day". They left the room. That was a change. The message is always drink 8 glasses of water a day.

I decided to only have a drink of water with medication. The medication was Panadol and Hydrocortisone tablets. Hydrocortisone is given after this type of surgery. The pituitary gland is the master gland: it tells all the other glands which hormones to produce. We automatically produce hydrocortisone in a stressful situation. This is the fight or flight hormone. It is given as a precaution in case the body cannot do it.

For now I just keep saying....

All is well. Everything is working for my highest good.
Out of this situation only good will comes.
I am safe all is well. Amen.

This little poem is from "You can heal your life" - Louise L Hay, so going to give it my best shot.

Not long until Christmas?

The days were generally ok with plenty distractions and visitors ...... the nights. Keep busy between sleep. Practised the following: Healing codes [1]; Tapping [2;] alternative nostril breathing [3;] Yoga mudras[4] and Yoga Nidra [5;] Physical exercises [6]; Positive affirmations [7;] all good.

The nights were awful. I had difficulty sleeping.
When I did sleep, in my dreams I am in an engine room somewhere, and there is oil dripping everywhere. Last night there were motorbikes in the dream, and I am turning around and around on them. I am also kicking things over and knocking the nurses out of the way. It could be I am trying to get away from it all?

December 12 2013

Pages hi. Well another night over its 6.30 am. First half of night I had no sleep, second half better 2 – 4.40. Slept great for me, even when at home?? Nitrates down I can drink more??Salt levels stable which is fab? a couple of ?? Here and there grateful?

Not a good night's sleep, for parts of the night, if at all. I was pleased if I got any sleep as the above showed. I was always relieved when the morning came. At least 6.30 a.m., even in the dark mornings the night was done. The staff would change. As shown above my salt levels were down so more liquid allowed. I sometimes got a cup of tea and toast brought to me from one of the night staff before they went off duty.

"Here is your first breakfast of the day, enjoy" they would laugh. Breakfast was sometime around 8 o'clock, a long time for me to wait for a drink and food. When breakfast did come it was usually lovely creamy yoghurt, cereal, and toast. Very enjoyable, and I would feel better.

December 13 2013

How's my daughter doing with?

No kids were allowed on the ward for a few days. I remember the staff thought there might be a tummy bug problem….you know what I mean. When they get the all clear, the ward will be out of quarantine.
 I hoped that Tyler, my now oldest grandson, could come to see me. In the end it was decided it was not a good idea. I miss him so much.

? mild. Capsule/Tablets better to swallow all hurdles to overcome. My challenges soon ready for a BA.

No idea what this was about? Something about medication, capsules easier to swallow. I did ask at some point what the tablets were for. I have said about the hydrocortisone, the other tablets were Panadol.
"Why do I need them" I asked. I hated taking any medication.
"For the pain" said the nurse.
"I don't have any pain" I replied.
"That's because you are taking the meds".
"Ok but can I stop taking them" I asked.
"Of course, if you would rather not" responded the nurse.
I never took any more after that and surprisingly wasn't in any pain. The only problem, I was unable to move well.
There was a picture opposite my bed on the wall. It was my new grandson Bude. As I looked at it, I thought, he and I have something in common. We've both got to build our muscles up. We've got to be able to sit up unaided. We need to build strength in our feet legs and arms. For Bude, all over his body. For me, the left side of my body. At the minute we were both lying down on our backs. Babies, develop from the brain down their bodies developing muscle strength in the first year. For me, the surgeon said "the foot and leg will regain feelings first, then the arm, hand etc. and eventually the eye will open". It seems this is how it is after a bleed during an operation, symptoms of a stroke. Apart from the leg and arm challenge. I talked nonstop. When my sister came to visit she told me to shut up
 "Stop talking! You talk all the time; I can't get a word in edgeways!" She had always been the talker and I the listener.

It seemed my face had dropped on one side. I never looked in the mirror because I couldn't see clearly, so didn't realise. I say didn't realise but my back teeth felt strange, like they weren't lined up properly and it was easy for me to bite my cheek. It was a long time later in January when the Endocrine Doctor said "Your face is looking symmetrical now."

"What did the Doctor mean about my face" I asked John when we came out of the hospital. "Yes your face was lopsided and your mouth had dropped", he said. "So I did have a stroke?" "Well glad I have improved" I said sarcastically.

The brains down so hopefully had? Clean night.
?deodorant to, John be here soon be ought that time now? staff here. If I? Pick a team could never have picked better than this crew.

Think this was about being neurologically tired as well as physically. It seems it takes ages to recover from surgery. For every hour on the operation table takes one month to recover.
The above was about needing some deodorant. Not the usual. I wanted a natural product. Stefanie brought some from "Neal's Yard" a shop in the Arcade in Newcastle which sold all natural products. Stefanie got a lavender deodorant. I felt throughout my stay in hospital that I smelt. I remember apologising to Natasha the Physiotherapist.
"You do not smell, and anyway it's a hospital there are a lot of smells" she said.
John came to visit every day and stayed all day and helped me with eating and other stuff. I felt better when he was there and would nod off to sleep. The rest of this gibberish is my appreciation of all the staff.

"What's that lovely smell" enquired my named nurse as she came into my room.
"It's lavender". I replied. "New deodorant" I continued
"When one of my visitors comes in to see me, they ran my spare face cloth under cold water, rang it out until nearly dry, and then dropped lavender oil onto it. As it dries the aroma evaporates into the air, yes it smells nice and relaxing" I continued,
"Lavender is a healing essential aromatherapy oil, so good to use in a sick room".
"I like coming into your room, apart from smelling nice it's so calm and peaceful" she said.
"Oh, it will be my healing crystals on the table and the angel cards".

I brought these items with me when I came into hospital to help the healing process. The cards were Archangel Raphael, the healing angel, and Archangel Michael to protect me and give me strength.

"The healing energy is brought by my healing angels, my friends. They bring it with them on their visits. It gives me and the room a sense of peace and calm".

"You nurses are my nursing angels. Thank you and God bless you all".

Chapter Eight

8 "Under the corner of the house, two feet were sticking out"

December 14 2013

Walked, walked and walked into the en-suite…. getting better. Yesterday the nurse said "I think you can walk today" as she helped me out of bed. So we gave it a try. It was strange because my left leg and foot didn't know what to do so we moved them and dragged them until they got the message. I had had a better night, slept 4 hours, and good for me. Restless for the rest of night, but got pleasure and joy from the fact I walked the previous day. Now with help this morning I walked. I was now sitting up in the chair. John will be pleased. Stefanie is coming today so good to go, and our Liz as well will ask her what progress she making with house.

Writer in residence today. Shower good. Good NHS very? with the Royal Victoria Infirmary here in Newcastle.

If I was given the choice of care, in this hospital, I could not have picked a better group of staff, medical or otherwise. Kind caring, compassionate, I've got all the time in the world for them. Our Claire's sister-in-law works in St George's Hospital in London. She said that the RVI had the best Neurology department, surgeons and staff and she was right.

December 15 2013

6.00 am Morning pages. Got through another night. Getting better all the time. Slept well?? Picking up and? Moving on the bed a bit feel better then

Well pages, had breakfast, had shower, had hair washed and dried. Now sitting in the chair for longer and longer each day so that's good. My brother brought me in a "Chair Topper" and now sitting comfortably and not slipping down in the leather seat.
And getting more confident sitting up, don't feel as sickly as I did when I first sat in it. John will be here soon at 11 o'clock. I am content now for a bit. Walking more now with help and I am getting stronger each day. I will sit here till lunch. I ordered roast chicken etc., and apple crumble and custard.

Good food considering my diet is gluten free, why people complain I don't know.

Floor? room, cool just right from me. Drink on table, cranberry, apple and blackcurrant. Need new flavour now. Got lots of cake and? writing pad and? sink in the room.
 # 27 2+7=9 good # one and a half weeks till Christmas. Sunday? Steve Wright love songs, Terry Wogan at 11o'clock? Johnnie Walker, Paul O'Grady etc. If lucky might get to see results of Strictly Come Dancing. Feel normal. Hair dried with drier by nurse, feel more normal.

It seems it must be a Sunday. The gibberish talks about programs on the radio. Sunday love songs with Steve Wright. Terry Wogan at 11 and the afternoon radio shows. I always listened at home so enjoyed the familiarity and normality of the radio.
 I feel emotionally good from time to time. When John visits he is bringing in my Kindle, I will put my glasses on, do some Sudoku if possible. I have done my healing routine: Healing Codes, tapping, pranayama breathing, Yoga Asana, Yoga Nidra as well as mudras. This was all in the hope that I could retrain the left side of my body arm, hand and fingers, leg, foot and toes to move again. It seems the left side has lost the memory of how to move because of the bleed on the right side of my brain. It all keeps me busy when I cannot sleep. I use my right hand and physically move that particular part of my left side a million times a night and day. And no I am not making it up I do it a lot of times. Only way to go if I want to not only get out of this bed by myself but also walk to the loo on my own and be able to do what is needed for me. Mainstream medicine has done its bit, others have done their bit, and it's now up to me to recover from the surgery and what has happened because of it.

I rest my head on a neck cushion.
"A big thank you, Tyler."
The neck cushion belongs to my now eldest grandson Tyler he lent it to me. It's pink and orange and it represents a caterpillar butterfly so I reckon it's the new me who will come out of the chrysalis into a butterfly when I get through this. It's comfortable, I lie on it on my right side because, to put my head straight onto the pillow involves pressing on the fourteen stitches on that side of my head.

Oh God Help me?? Or someone, this is awful I want to go home, I want to go home.

I cried as the tears fell on the pages.

Stephen Hawkins believes that, "In every black hole there is light" and I think now that he is right because here in my black hole, I need compassion for myself. Not to be so hard on myself, it's not my own fault this has happened to me. Or is it? We get what we wish for, but why did I wish for this.

I have had enough now. To quote Dorothy in the Wizard of Oz: "There is no place like home". That's the problem. My feet cannot click together, they have forgotten how to. Maybe it's because I am not wearing ruby slippers? Not wearing any slippers.

"Put your slippers on" said the nurse when I began to walk.
"No thank you, I find it difficult to walk with slippers on.
"Without them I can feel the floor and that makes it easier" I replied.

That's why I am still in hospital? My feet need more training and a bit of magic. Going to keep up my healing routine and positive thoughts, that lot will keep me and my brain busy. I got a brain, got certificates to prove it. Poor, poor thing, it is so tired needs a rest.

Chapter Nine

9 "Somewhere over the rainbow"

Just like Scarecrow in The Wizard of Oz, he and I were on the yellow brick road to get a brain for him and get my old brain back. We should have been in Australia by now. John and Tony were going to the Ashes; they had the tickets for the Boxing Day Test Match. Christmas Eve was to be in Melbourne's Botanical Gardens. I began to cry, I just wanted to go home. I had had enough.

I was told the weather was proving mild for December, here in the north of England. The snow was keeping off. No white Christmas here this year.
 "If you do get home for Christmas" John said "I will make the Christmas dinner because it will be lovely if you are home". He continued "We got a lovely new telly so Christmas programmes will look good on it".
I thought people can call in to see me, if they want to. Wait and see what's what. Not the Christmas planned I thought as I sobbed gently… hey ho. I was alive…wasn't I?

John was bringing in his laptop with the videos which Claire and Tony kept sending us of Bude, our new grandchild. Oh the joys of modern technology. In the past, when people emigrated anywhere in the world, never mind Australia, it was months before relatives back home, received a letter. These days we are so lucky with the internet, Skype and virtual reality. I am so looking forward to John coming in.

December 16 2013

6 a.m. ….. Hi pages. Another night over. Alice, the nurse, was a godsend at 12 midnight. I didn't feel too good, hot. I wondered if my temperature was up. I was worried about the rest of the night ahead. Alice took my temperature, it was normal, but she was good to me and got me a cold compress, she also put cool gel on my head. Then she also showed me how I could have light on and switch it off when I needed to with the on/off button. I had been in hospital all these weeks and no-one had shown me this switch. I felt so much better knowing this. Thank you Alice and for tea and toast at 6 a.m., the real breakfast wouldn't arrive until around 8 o'clock.

December 16 2013

Progress now. Walking time to sort? Progress. John is in and maybe transferring to Hexham, nearer to home?
Well pages I walked along the corridor and back with the support of Natasha the physiotherapist. What an achievement today. Yippee Aye.

Dec ember 17 2013

7am No sleep, but coping better with the night. Night time Radio 2 programmes are brilliant to pass the night away to. Tony Blackburn has a good show.
Motown 10-11, comedy 11 -12 after 12 then Vanessa and now Chris Evans' early morning shows on. The only way is up. At 9.21am had a proper bath. Mandy one of the nurses took me along to a different bathroom, lovely, lovely. She helped me onto a seat which she lowered into the bath. First bath in three or four weeks, it was heaven. Thank you nurse Mandy.

Sitting in chair at table waiting for breakfast – here it comes, yoghurt, toast orange juice. John will be here. God hasn't finished with me yet. Best is yet to come.

Reader as you can see, I wrote a lot about my nights and breakfast, but wrote much less about the rest of the day.
The nights were the worst for me. I was not relaxed enough to get to sleep. I wasn't a good sleeper at home either. There might have been a lot of reasons for this; I could not get comfortable in the plastic single hospital bed; I slept on my back because I was unable to sleep on my left side, couldn't feel it; couldn't get comfortable on my right side. Stitches in my head were uncomfortable. After this kind of operation patients are automatically given hydrocortisone medication just in case the pituitary gland doesn't work. That medication is part of the fight or flight we need in case of danger, I might have been producing my own at this point which might result in having too much in my body. During the night I felt powerless, lonely and very frightened. Breakfast was the end of the night and the beginning of the day. After breakfast I was helped to get dressed, which involved two nurses getting me out of bed and helping me into a wheel chair. Pushing me into the bathroom and helping me to shower etc. I was pushed back into my room and helped onto the chair for a while. I found sitting up in this hospital chair difficult and could sit only for a short time. I would do my writings and try to do Sudoku then I would get help back to bed. The doctors did their rounds, and then John would come in to see me. Then it was lunch time. Either

before lunch or after lunch I would catch up on my sleep because I felt safe when John was there. The afternoons were visiting and either family our Liz or friends-most times Kate -would visit. John would go and get lunch at this point or would go for coffee and man chat. Mandy, and Liz Weir came and they would kindly give me a treatment, Shiatsu or Energy Healing. Thank you my healing angels. The days were busy with comings and goings. In the evening either Stefanie or David would visit me. Before they left they all made sure I had enough little snacks, either fruit or a biscuit or little gluten free cake, which I held back from tea. These snacks were on my table over the bed and in easy reach, all helping me get me through the night. John would be taken home by either David or Stefanie. Then it was night again. This was my life for about four weeks in the R. V.I.

Chapter Ten

10 "Follow the yellow brick road"

December 18 2013

We are going to transfer you to Hexham General" said the charge nurse.
"No" I said, tears rolling down my cheeks. "I want to go home".
"I have had enough".
"Of course you can go home if you want to, but we feel you will improve your mobility if you go to Hexham". She continued:
"Hexham is a good hospital for physiotherapy and you will benefit if you have some physiotherapy".

Again I requested to go home instead of Hexham. I've got a big bed at home, en-suite, recliner Ikea chair, I will be fine. At home I will see Tyler.... missing him now. The medical folk were worried that I could be house-bound. I lived in a first floor flat with no lift. There were two flights of stairs to climb. At Hexham General I could be trained and gain confidence to scale the stairs. I agreed to go.

Today we were going to Skype Claire. Watch baby Bude having his bath. Joy of joys he is lovely. I can smell him, that baby smell.

England lost Ashes in Australia. John did not miss anything out there at the Melbourne Cricket Ground (MCG) in Melbourne.

December 19 2013

Not good overnight. It's getting light now, dayshift coming on and hopefully scrambled eggs. John will be here soon. I was cold overnight and getting desperate for breakfast. So very tired. Need to sleep but cannot get comfy in bed. Need to be home on my own settee. I will nod off easily comfortable in front of the telly. Tired! Tired! so very tired.

They will assess my mobility at Hexham. See how I am and hopefully go home for Christmas. Tearful, tired, despondent now had enough. Hurry up

John. I wait to find out more when people know more. Be home for Christmas. Need to sleep now.

December 19 2013

Going to Hexham 2.00pm. I was going home by default. We had to pass it to get to the hospital.

The journey in the ambulance was awful for me I was sitting up, seat belt on, but because of the weakness in my left side I felt very unsafe. I put my distress down to no sleep, and moving without a familiar face. I was very upset and began crying.

As I looked out of the window for the first time in the real world I realised my eyesight wasn't good. By the time I got to the hospital I felt really low. I was admitted. My new room was lovely. Not as clinical as before. It still had the usual bed, chair, wash basin etc. The soft furnishings were the harlequin pattern. The of colours red, orange and yellow. I sat on my own for what seemed ages. I thought John wasn't far behind but it was a long while before he arrived. In fact I became very distressed and I didn't have my phone or any numbers to see where he was. Doctors came and went. I felt so alone and out of control all I did was cry. The doctor assured me my state was natural in view of being transported to a hospital I didn't know, outside my comfort zone. I laugh now because someone took a blood sample to check blood sugar levels and that prick was the most pain I had experienced in all of the days and weeks I was in the RVI. I was such a cry baby. It seems John had waited for Stefanie to give him and my stuff a lift to Hexham. I left RVI at 12.30. John hadn't appeared by 2 pm, I thought he was following behind and would be there when I arrived. I was scared, worried, and sobbing couldn't stop. The doctor reassuringly told me it was OK to feel how I felt. I had been moved out of my comfort zone to somewhere new with no familiar faces around me.

December 20 2013

7am well pages. Better night here at Hexham. Slept 8-10 p.m. had supper of sandwich and Bakewell tart and drink. Went back to sleep and slept till 1 a.m. I was awakened by Bridget the night nurse to introduce herself. Although I thought another long night ahead I felt better for the sleep. For the rest of the night I did my healing recovery routine. Felt comfortable, much better. It was better than the previous night, no sleep at all.

I am now sitting here at the table, writing. Morning routine finished. John will be coming in at 11.a.m, I've got my glasses on and they are helping with my eye sight. I still see only with one eye. Better chair here at Hexham everything so comfortable. With this decor of red, orange and yellow, it all feels cosy even the bed.

Feeling a great improvement today, getting better all the time. My time here has not been wasted. By the time I am discharged will be ready to go home and it will not be a problem. Breakfast was good. It was cornflakes, better than the Rice Krispies, with raisins/bananas and a glass orange juice. Sitting up tall, the table is the right height. The drinking cup is manageable. It is plastic, lightweight and with a big handle. The toast arrived after a prompt, its gluten free bread so have to ask for it was delicious.

I am ready for physiotherapy today. I thought to myself.
"I am so pleased with myself". I can now do stomach crunches, sit ups from the lying position…. been practising every night in RVI and now here at Hexham. I have been practising holding opposite side of table with challenged hand. Bit of a struggle but my aim is to keep doing it to strengthen the muscles in my left hand/arm etc. "Oh, bugger". The table is stuck. I will leave that exercise till later when it's unstuck. I practice moving the table with my challenged hand/arm. I move the table to different angle. The stretch helps my arm. I can do sit ups now. Sitting here in this chair, I can see outside the window. There is smoke blowing from a chimney. There is also a gentle swaying of the trees in the breeze, normality has returned.

Chapter Eleven

11 "Beginning of the yellow brick road"

It was good in Hexham General. The staff were lovely, both night and day staff, as well as other non-medical staff. I received physiotherapy and was shown how to get the left side of my body moving better. One of the exercises I did was the wipe on/wipe off routine. Wipe off in circles with the left hand, wipe on in circles with the right hand. You know what I mean, if you have ever seen Karate Kid. I also had to practise my squats - up and down, up and down. I was very fit before the surgery so doing these excises wasn't a problem and the doing of them was to send new messages and create new memories to another part of my brain, the muscles were toned. This was done every day while I was there. The place was less clinical than RVI- it was a bit of a cottage hospital. One of the days my grandson of 5 and half came to visit, the first time we had seen each other in 6 weeks. John pushed me in a wheelchair via the lift down stairs to the reception area and I sat excitedly waiting for him to come through the rotating door with his mum Stefanie.

"Grandma, Grandma" he called as he came through the door. "Hello darling, come and sit on granny's knee". His mum picked him up as I couldn't. I could have cried but not in front of the bairn.

"What have you got?" I said.

"Here Grandma, I brought Hearty to see you and give you a cuddle". Hearty was a red heart shaped cushion, with long arms at either side. Tyler loved this cushion he took it everywhere and people would smile, point, and say

"Ah look, he's carrying his heart".

"He carries his heart with him everywhere" I would reply.

This visit from Tyler and Hearty was needed. I had realised that my heart was broken. Not only, because of what I was going through, but also, because I never got to Australia. Just like the Tin Man I needed a new heart. This visit from my grandson was the start.

Other visits and visitors came. One evening my sister visited. She brought joy in the form of crisp sandwiches. My tastes had changed and sis said,

"Next time I come let's have a picnic in the reception area". We all loved picnics.

"Good idea" we all chanted.

The reception area was a great place, a bit like an airport, brightly lit; the furniture was covered with the same harlequin décor. There were tables, chairs and comfortable armchairs. On the walls hung paintings, depicting sea views, some depicting waves lashing about. The ceilings were high, with sky windows in the day giving a lot of light. We giggled like naughty kids, gathering seats around a table and while sitting comfortably. John went for tea from the machine, Liz made the sandwiches and the icing on the cake was David and Laura arriving - fabulous. We had such a good evening it was dark outside but we didn't notice. I felt normality had returned.

It was nearly Christmas. On another day we, that's me, John, David and Laura joined other patients and staff members for a Christmas party. I even won the raffle. A child sang.....we all joined in and sang Christmas carols. We ate a Christmas tea (which was our usual hospital tea).

I was at Hexham General for only 4 days but it all helped in my recovery and a feeling of "I can do this it will be alright."

Chapter Twelve

12 "There is no place like home"

December 23 2013

My walking had improved somewhat, and It was agreed that I could go home in time for Christmas, so today was the day. I was discharged. "Have a Merry Christmas and a Happy New Year" said the staff.

We were off. "You don't need an ambulance" the charge nurse said to John "she will be ok with you; you could wait ages for one". Bye-bye.

"We are on our own now" said John.

"Well not quite" said the nurse as she pushed me in the wheelchair to the hospital entrance helped me into the car and we were off, scary stuff.

"We will manage fine" said John, thrilled as I was because the nurses thought we would be able to cope.

"Yes "I replied as we drove off.

"We will see still got two flights of stairs to get up"

Got home and who should be there to greet us, but Stefanie and Tyler. We enlisted them both to get upstairs. Stefanie behind in case I fell back with Tyler in front to lead the way, he thought it was great to be able to help and so did I. John was at my left side with the bannister on my right I could hold it as I carefully climbed the stairs one by one.

Chapter Thirteen

13 "Can you help me find my way?"

December 24 2013

Christmas Eve was very busy with visitors: Stefanie, Tyler, David, Laura, my brother Allan and my niece Rachel, and Kate my long-time friend and her husband Paddy.

"Do you want any last minute shopping" asked my daughter in law Laura Jane.

"No thank you. I did all of the Christmas shopping in June and July, remember? We were supposed to be going to Australia! Went to hospital instead, but see I was well prepared for either event", I said laughing and crying at the same time with tears of happiness rolling down my cheeks.

Off they all went, some home, and others to finish their own shopping. It was Christmas Eve and with everyone gone John and I were going to have our meal and open our presents to each other. We have done this for years. It started when the kids were small and no baby sitters on Christmas Eve to go out so John and I started our own tradition. Meal, bottle of wine and open a present, the beginning of Christmas for us. As the kids got older each was allowed to join in with this ritual. Happy memories. Very sad…. sniffling and crying….we were supposed to be in the Botanic Gardens in Melbourne singing carols with Claire, Tony and the new baby, in warm conditions in the middle of an Australian summer. Heartbroken! Now here we were sitting in our house on a cold winter Christmas evening….and realised no presents or even cards for each other because we were going to shop for them in Australia. We looked at each other through the tears and smiled through it all as we realised we had a present to give……each other…what else was there to give? "Merry Christmas" we said as we raised our glasses of non-alcoholic wine. We were now crying tears of joy so glad to be here, we had each other. What the future had in store didn't matter it was Christmas Eve 2013 and we were alive.

Chapter Fourteen

14 "The wind shrieked, and the whole house shook"

Stefanie's story

October 2013

I texted Mum. Tyler had wanted to go to her house for tea. She rang me back and said,
"No car."
She had been to the opticians and had been told that she may have tunnel vision".
"No driving for the time being".
I looked up what might cause this and there was a list of causes that couldn't have had anything to do with it– one was alcohol consumption, another was hallucinogenic drugs, another was a bite from a Black Mamba snake.
However one cause was a pituitary tumour.

November 5 2013
Mum had an appointment at the hospital. She was told that she had a tumour on her pituitary gland and would need an operation. I was at work at the time and mum rang me to tell me. I came off the phone, went back into the office and burst into tears while telling the girls. They made me go home. I couldn't have concentrated for the rest of the day.

November 26 2013

I took Tyler to school, went home and waited for dad to ring to say mum had gone down for her op. The only thing I could concentrate on was a table runner I was making for sewing class. Dad rang about 10.30am. He said,
"Operation will take between 3 and 4 hours".
He would ring again when mum came out.

Dad rang later to say mum was out and on the High Dependency Unit. He was at the hospital and staying there until he could go in and see her. He rang

again about 6pm and. said mum was really groggy, but OK. Not to come in –
stay with Tyler.

November 27 2013

I went into work as usual despite it being the last place I wanted to be. I
knew Dad was going to see Mum, and I texted him about 9.30am to say I
would meet him off the bus and I was coming in with him. I asked my boss
if it was OK and just managed to get out the words.
"My mum had an operation yesterday and I want to go and see her",
I said, before I started crying as I was rushed off to the toilets.

We had been told by the doctors that Mum would be in hospital for a week,
home to recover for a couple of weeks and would be able to fly a month after
the operation. So, when I went in to see her wasn't prepared for what I saw.
I immediately burst into tears and I remember thinking,
"You stupid girl this isn't helping anyone".
Poor Mum, her head was covered with a bandage and she was hooked up to
the machines but she still managed to say
"I'm still in here somewhere"

We stayed for a while but then we had to get back to work. I was still in tears
so Dad made me sit down. I remember saying to him that Mum sounded
really angry even though she was saying nice things. I also remember
thinking Mum's mouth didn't look right but I couldn't figure out why.

28 November 2013

I went in to the hospital that night. Mum had had the bandage removed and
looked a little less scary.

Dad was going to the hospital every day for about 11 o'clock. Mum wasn't
eating very well and every day we would take different things in for her to try.
She now was enjoying sandwich spread sandwiches, fruit pots, Heinz tomato
soup, things she never ate before.

She was too hot in bed and when she was sitting on the chair she was scared
she was going to slip off. We took some "Kool" strips in to help cool her
down. We must have tried everything to make it more comfortable for her. I
think Neal's Yard, Boots, Morrison's, Asda, Sainsbury's, Tesco did a roaring
trade.

David and I took turns going in to visit each night, as well as being there to give Dad a lift back home. If it wasn't my night to visit I always made Dad come into my house so he could touch base and give me an update on how Mum was. It was a chance for me to see if either of them needed anything. I didn't want him to go straight home from the hospital and be by himself.

Sunday 1 December
Tyler hadn't seen his Grandma for nearly a week. Mum suggested I took a photo from her 'good side', to show him. On the photo Mum is waving at the camera. It must have taken all her strength to do that.

Tues 3 December

Dad rang me tonight to say Claire had gone into labour. I was so excited. It was just the good news we needed.

Wed 4 December
I was at work when, at about 11am our time, my phone rang. It said Claire on the display but I thought it would be Tony actually calling. I said hello and then Claire said "you've got a new nephew".

Friday 6 December
Mum and Dad had ordered a new telly and it was due to be delivered today. I went and house sat for them. I took all the things I needed to do my Christmas table runner I was making. I just got there, all set up when the doorbell rang and the telly was there.

Saturday 7 December
I needed some edging for my runner so I thought I would go into town, do a bit of shopping and then go in to see Mum. After my shopping I went in to see Mum. I had my runner with me and Mum asked to see it.

Approx. 10 December
Mum and Dad had been told that Mum might be getting transferred to Hexham hospital soon. I thought this was great news as when Dad was transferred to Hexham that was the last stage before coming home. Mum didn't want to go to another hospital. She just wanted to go home. A few days later there was a sickness and diarrhoea bug on the ward and no patients were allowed in or out.

Tuesday 19 December

Mum was told she would be transferring to Hexham that day. She went in an ambulance and I met Dad at the RVI to collect Mum's stuff and take them to Hexham. When I got there the Ward Sister was on her break and her office (where mum's stuff was) was locked. Dad and I chatted on while we waited for the sister to come back. One of the things Dad mentioned which he had just found out was that during the operation Mum had had bleed on her brain. This can cause some of the same symptoms as a stroke and explained why Mum's mouth had been droopy the day after the operation.

Dad headed off to Hexham and later, after I picked Tyler up from school, I went to visit in the evening.

Friday 20 December
Tyler was away from school, because of a training day. He had just bought a fuzzy talking toy called Ferby, as an early Christmas present (it was my bargain – a £55 toy reduced to £15). Mum and Dad came down to the café part and we sat and chatted and Tyler showed off his new toy.

Monday 23 December
The physiotherapist at the hospital had arranged for some equipment to be delivered to help when Mum came home. Tyler and I went and house sat. Dad rang mid-morning and said Mum was coming home today, they were just waiting for an ambulance to bring her. He then rang a little later and said that he had been told he could bring Mum home if they felt comfortable doing that.

About an hour later Mum and Dad pulled up outside the front door. We all helped mum up the stairs as she couldn't use her left side very well and couldn't see properly. But it was lovely to have her home.

Wednesday 1 January 2014

I had invited Mum and Dad for lunch. I went along and picked them up, because it took two people to help Mum down the stairs. I think they had a good time and it was nice for them to have a change of scenery. I was really proud of them both. It must have taken a tremendous effort to do it.

Part two

"Follow the Yellow Brick Road"

Chapter Fifteen

15 "On the horizon something sparkled"

Well Christmas and New Year came and went. We had a lot of visitors. We had a great day opening our Christmas presents as each family member arrived. All of their gifts were given at the beginning of November because we were going to Australia or Heaven. It was lovely to open our presents with others even if overshadowed we had a very happy day.

New Year's Eve ….we went to bed early… couldn't last past ten o'clock. New Year's Day was a good one. We went for New Year's Lunch with Stefanie, Jamie and Tyler at their house. It was the first time out and although a bit scary what with the journey, going up and down stairs in both my flat and Stefanie's house and managing to use cutlery to eat dinner with, I enjoyed the company and Tyler took great delight in showing his Christmas presents. I gave myself a pat on the back for the challenges and achievements of the day. During the two weeks holiday Stefanie came to our house most days to help out and do what she could. David did any fetching and carrying and cheering up his dad, who was finding it all a bit too much, but we got through it all.

Chapter Sixteen

16 "The Wicked Witch of the North"

January 2014

"We will need a scan", the endocrine doctor said.

"Why?" I responded.

"To see everything is ok" he continued, also "There is a need for a blood test".

"What's that all about?" I asked.

"You have been on hydrocortisone since your operation"

"Yes and why is that?"

"It's about the pituitary gland which is the controller gland of all the other glands in the body and there was a chance after the surgery your hydrocortisone hormones might be lacking. Let's have a test, see how your levels are; you might be producing your own. This hormone is the fight or flight hormone. Your moods will be affected if you have too much".

"Well that would explain why John and I are arguing all the time?"

I didn't feel strong enough to go through all these medical things. The doctor also suggested I might want to see a psychologist to help me come to terms with my new situation?

"We got out the entire tumour no need for another operation" said the surgeon a few days after the surgery. I continued

"Why a scan?" I had one following the operation".

"We just want to check" said the doctor.

"You might find other tumours" I replied.

"No" the doc responded. "And that eye, we might need to operate to open it".

"No! No more operations." And don't need the counselling, I like a challenge. I will be fine".

Every time I went to the hospital it was always something else to worry about. We went for a cup of tea and I cried. When will all this end? The specialist Sister did say at my first appointment "I'm Sister Miller and we will be seeing each other for the next year". So it looked like it was going to be a long road to recovery.

I also made an appointment to have a chat with the surgeon. I wanted to know if the pituitary gland had been removed during the operation.

On the appointment day it was not the surgeon who performed the operation. It was a different surgeon, who to be frank was rather brusque. He said that there was a chance there was no gland left. He also said briskly

"How you are at this point is probably how you will be for the rest of your life." He continued, "Your eyes will not improve".

At this stage the right eye was still closed. I felt so deflated by the time we left the interview. But hey ho what do they know.

Chapter Seventeen

17 "Scarecrow found a tree of nuts and filled Dorothy's basket with them, so she would not be hungry for a long time"

January 2014

January wasn't all bad.

"Come on Kath" said my daughter-in-law Laura.

"We are going to see our Charlie; she will make you feel better." Charlie was Laura's cousin and her job was in a local beauty shop, you know the thing, nails painted, facials and massages.

"No petal, I can't get out of here", meaning our flat. "Down two flights of stairs, never mind getting into your car."

This was a Renault Grand Scenic with a high step to climb up to get into the car.

"Don't pull the sick card Kath; I made the appointment so we're going, come on".

The fear is worse than the reality, as Susan Jeffers says in her book, "Feel the fear and do it anyway". Off we went. I walked down the two flights of stairs backwards, got in and out of the car with a gentle push. I thoroughly enjoyed the afternoon. Charlie was fabulous, obviously a people person. I had a full pedicure with massage and nail varnish as well as a manicure with massage and vanish. It came at the right time, very relaxing and beneficial for the movement of these limbs. I was there for hours, just what I needed. Our David picked us up, both Laura and I beautified, and she didn't want to smudge anything so he drove us home. On the way back, he pulled up outside the hairdressers in the village,

"Right Mam; let's sort out your hair". It needed sorting; it had not had anything done to it since before the operation. The surgery involved shaving the right side of my head and I still had some of the 14 stitches there and now scar tissue. David jumped back into the car.

"Ok Jason understands your situation and he can do you at 4.30 or tomorrow morning, ok".

So the next day I, with the help of John, got back down the stairs and into the car and off to the hairdressers. Jason was great he did a dry trim; I wasn't ready to let anyone else do a wash. I still had a lot of stitches in my head and if not there was scar tissue. Jason was gentle and kind and he understood.

"I've done people's hair with worse than what you got here". It looked fabulous, best dry trim ever, I looked good and I didn't have hair sticking up everywhere because Jason also blow dried it. Feeling like a million dollars now we went home and had a great meal prepared by John, life was good.

February 2014

February came, no word from hospital about tests etc.

"I would love a swim" I thought. I swam regularly before but now no chance of going to the local pool not on my own or even with any one. The left side of my body was not up to the job yet. The Neurological Physiotherapist was visiting each week and showing me exercises I could do to not only strengthen the muscles in my left arm and leg but also to send new messages back and forwards to a different part of the brain to teach the brain, arms and leg a new memory. It seems a discovery over the years was that the brain was not a solid thing but was pliable and new things could be learnt. So swimming was needed to teach the limbs to move- my daughter- in- law to the rescue. Laura and David were foster parents and they looked after children with all sorts of issues, disabilities being one of the issues.

"Swim? Swim?" said Laura with a puzzled look on her face.

"Come on, we're going out".

"Where are we going?" I asked.

"The Alan Shearer Activity Centre" she replied.

I knew the centre. Alan Shearer the footballer was its Founder. It was a charity run centre for children and adults with disabilities. They ran playgroups, all children welcome; I used to take our Tyler there. There is a large ball pool for all ages, sensory light and touch rooms as well as a café and a hydro therapy pool.

"Yes you're eligible" said the lady on reception following the completion of a form, which Laura did. We think they thought Laura was my carer. I could use the facility which consisted of a small heated pool, showers and changing rooms and all set in dimmed lighting. Fabulous. I booked every Tuesday and used it for three months. John would take me and we loved it. John enjoyed swimming but since his operation he was reluctant to go in the water in case of any accidents. So every Tuesday for three months this is what we did. We had the place to ourselves for an hour, which doesn't seem long but it was long enough. It proved to be a life saver, the warm water assisted my movements and by the end I could move my arms and legs- separately, and eventually together - to swim a few strokes.

Chapter Eighteen

18 "A spicy scent filled the air"

Therapies

Now I was to become the Chief Executive, Project Manager, and all other roles of people who had my best interests at heart. I was on my healing journey, my yellow brick road to wellness and 2014 was to be my recovery year and, like a scarecrow, the stuffing had been knocked out of me. Any surgery, major or minor, results in the body being out of balance for a while. My surgery was to my head and, like any other head injury, it's a big deal. Not only was my head still healing from the stitches, but also from the fact surgeons had to enter my head inside on the right side to get to the tumour and remove it. All surgery has side effects like any medication. There was a bleed during the operation which caused the left side of my body to be paralysed. There was also trauma to the nerves on the right side of my head going back and forwards to the brain from the right eye. This resulted in the right eye being closed. At this stage it was unable to open itself. I have a lot of questions over this? Why were there problems when the eye did open? Why the loss of field vision; the double vision; the lack of definition. Might it be because of the bleed during the operation? Even the trauma of the surgery could be the reason? The optic nerve damaged because the tumour had been pressing on it; the pituitary gland being disturbed? There were still many questions. Not sure of any answers, and still cannot get a satisfactory answer, maybe all of the above reasons. My niece is a clinical psychologist, working with people who have had head injuries. She assured me that eventually I would be alright. It was a long way to go down this yellow brick road to recovery.

The NHS is good at identifying disease and saving lives through surgery, but they cannot afford a lot of money for the recovery. I believe it's down to the patient to assist themselves in their own recovery. I was prepared to try any other healing modality I could find from anywhere around the world.

When in Hospital I was grateful to have received Energy Healing [1] from Liz Weir a good friend. After I was discharged she continued to treat me at my home. Liz is the CEO of Northumbria Healers in Riding Mill, Northumberland.

Another friend Mandy, a Shiatsu [2] practitioner also gave me treatments during this time. Both of these practices release of any energy blocked in the meridians, the energy centres of the body.

In Chinese medicine it is believed that blocked energy can be the reason for illness. I understand that these modalities of healing are all about moving the energy around the body and the release any blockages.

I continued to do the Tapping [3] which again is energy release and I could do it myself between treatments from others.

I continued with The Healing Codes [4] another energy healing system using the finger tips to move the energy to different areas of the head and neck. Though not totally understanding how any of it worked at this point, I kept going. I thought to myself I didn't know how electricity works but I switch on the lights and hay presto, light.

Claire Skyped most days not only to show us baby Bude, but also to see how I was doing.

"Mum, what about getting in touch with Dr Deepika". Dr Deepika Rodrigo is a friend of Claire's who is an Ayurvedic Doctor from Sri Lanka. Ayurveda is the traditional healing system from India. She is one of the people responsible for bringing Ayurvedic healing [5] to the UK. This form of healing is the sister of Yoga and as Claire is not only a yoga teacher but also a Yogi and training as an Ayurvedic practitioner, it was a good idea.

Claire continued "She will help you through your recovery."

So I decided to try Ayurvedic Healing.

I began to take different kinds of herbs and spices prescribed for me. There were herbs to help my digestion, herbs to relax me and help me sleep. The herbs which I could see the benefits of, were the herbal oils. I used them three times a day as a massage.

I massaged the oil onto my left arm and leg. In fact, I massaged it onto the whole left, motionless side of my body - It was for paralysis. The oil was also analgesic - good to use to ease the pain caused - as I tried to move the limbs. It was also good for rheumatism (if I had any). What did I have to lose? Maybe I would gain a lot.

"Rub it around your eye" said Dr Deepika

"It will help it to open your eye" she continued at our Skype consultation.

I did it morning, noon and night. I so desperately wanted my right eye to open. The consultant at the hospital said that an operation might be needed to open it. I was determined that I wouldn't go through any other surgery

As the year rolled on I also had Ayurvedic Indian head massages and full body massages. These were given to me by a lady called Glynis. Glynis is an Ayurvedic therapist in massage as well as a yoga teacher [6] and much, much more.

Deepika, Glynis, Liz and Mandy were my Angels of Healing. I thought of each of them as the witch Glinda from Oz. They got me through a lot.

The NHS did provide therapists. One was the Occupational, the other the Neurological, two lovely ladies. The Neurological Therapist came once a week for about half an hour for six weeks. She showed me what I needed to do to get the muscles working again in my left toes, foot and leg, as well as my arm hand and fingers. She thought I was doing a good job, practise all week until she came again. She said,

"It's down to you Kath that your mobility is improving. I tell you what to do, but you do the work" she continued

"If you do not want to lose it, use it".

What she meant was that I should walk around practising swinging my left arm, rather than holding it bent at the elbow against my chest. This was very good advice. At the beginning of my recovery, in my mind, the left side of my body seemed not to be part of me. Being positive, I called it my challenged side or challenged arm/leg, never my bad side. It's all about the words and thoughts we use which gives us a positive outcome. I would also repeat positive statements e.g. "I am strong, healthy, healed and whole".

"I move forward with ease and with love".

Also "My eye opens easily and effortlessly".

Saying these statements gave me a lift.

They came from a book "You can heal your life". [9]

As time went on and my mobility improved I got to a place where I integrated the left side of my body back into the whole of my body and I never gave it another thought. I was whole and complete.

The occupational therapist brought me activities, such as a peg, to strengthen my wrist, hand and fingers.

"The small muscles take a bit longer". She said.

It's amazing how opening and closing a peg can bring strength.

During January and February ...... my sister Liz came to stay with me each day whilst John went to work. One particular morning on awakening I didn't feel particularly strong, but our Liz was coming. Also this morning when I awoke, and opened my left eye, joy of joys, my right eye lid began to move. I could see slightly, day light through my now moving eyelashes.... My eye was beginning to open.

Chapter Nineteen

19 "Visitors from OZ"

February 13 2014

"Mam, can you and Dad be at our David's on Sunday" said Claire.

"Course we can, but why?"

"Just call in for a cuppa with me, Tony and baby Bude" she said exasperatedly?

"What do you mean?" I asked further.

"Come on Mam, wake up! We're flying home on Sunday, so is that a date?"

The penny dropped.

"Yes course we can" I said jumping up and down with excitement. It was our usual weekly Skype but never in a million years did I ever think this chat would be so exciting. Having said that, it was always exciting to talk to them and even more so since they had had the baby.

"Do David and Laura know you're coming?" I continued.

"Of course" she replied laughing "we've been arranging it for a couple of weeks, a bit of a surprise".

"Yippee aye" I screamed at the telly screen. In a few days I would see them and be able to touch and hug them as well as give that lovely little baby a cuddle so of course I began to cry tears of joy.

"Oh Claire, that's fab to see you all in a few days. Can't wait, how am I going to get through the next few days?"

"On cloud nine" replied Tony. We all laughed.

Now here we are sitting in the car outside our David's house.....I looked at the window and there they were standing in full view, Claire, Tony and being held by them... the miracle child Bude. We rushed into the house hugging each other laughing and crying at the same time and trying to talk through the tears.

It was a wonderful few weeks and it certainly lifted my and everyone else's spirits. We went out all over the place.

"I will push the pram" I said to Tony.

"Why?" he asked

"Because I am the granny and I have rights". I continued

"You see Tony, Bude is asleep and I get the pleasure as granny. As Dad, when he wakes up, you get the pain in figuring out why he is crying".

Because they lived in Australia they were not used to anyone asking to push the pram, so Tony was surprised at my request. Anyway, pushing the pram steadied my walking which was getting better day by day.

We had a family get together with brothers and sisters, aunts, uncles and cousins - even Bude's Great Grandpa at aged 88 was pleased to have this new addition to the family.

Only down side was at first I was, very nervous of lifting or holding the baby - the left arm wasn't yet strong enough to lift him or hold his weight and the right side was shaky, which was all about me really. Tony was kind, he encouraged me to help him with nappy changing etc. and my confidence grew. Claire gave me some Indian head and body massages as she was trained in these areas. With seeing them and the family altogether I felt much, much better. I never thought I would ever see this situation again.

We even went swimming. Guess where? The Alan Shearer Centre. We were allowed up to 7/8 people in the pool together. "Mum this is great" said Claire as she could see my progress. We only Skyped, and I was always sitting so, to see me in action was great for her. Claire, in the past was a swimming instructor in America on one of her University summers.

"Try hopping through the water" she said.

"Never mind Mum, keep practising and eventually you will be able to do it".

Yet another challenge.

It was such fun. We got to spend time together laughing and happy. Tyler showed off his new swimming skills and of course splashing his Grandad. Tony got to do swimming with his new baby Bude. Back in Australia it was Claire who took him swimming. Such good memories were made.

One of the gatherings was again at the home of David and Laura's. It was a wintery afternoon in February in the UK and the light of the day was diminishing. I was sitting in front of their log fire which gave of a lot of warmth with a fabulous wood burning smell and red crackling amber. Alfie, their black Labrador dog (spelt backwards GOD), was curled up on the mat in front of the fire. It was so very lovely and relaxing. I nodded off to sleep in the chair but still awake a bit to listen to the happy chatter and laughter. All this excitement ….I heard Claire's voice through it all.

"Mam you awake?" "Yes pet just resting my eyes". My right eye was slightly open now so I rested it when I could.

"Here's a little belated Christmas present from Australia for you"

I opened my eyes. Around me stood everyone, my hubby, my grown up children, their spouses, my oldest grandson Tyler and newest grandson being held, all grinning at me.

"What's all this about?"

Claire handed me a little package. As I opened it I could see tears and hear sobbing.

There in my hand was a pair of ruby sequined slippers.

As I put the slippers on my feet Claire said "Bought them for you for Christmas, but as you couldn't come over at that time… here they are".

"Oh they fit perfectly" said Claire.

I stood up looked at them all; my family all here and because of course I could do it now? I clicked my heels together three times while saying,

"There's no place like home. There's no place like home. There is no place like home".

Eventually, Claire, Tony and baby had to go back to Australia. There were a lot of us at the airport to say our goodbyes - very sad. It seemed like they had been here a short time but now, time to go back. It had been so special and helped me further along the yellow brick road to recovery.

Chapter Twenty

20 "Do you think Oz would give me courage?" asked the cowardly Lion"

March, the month of appointments for scan and tests. I was scared to go through with them, still feeling weak and wobbly. I had more strength than I realised. The scan was OK, just a bit noisy, and on the same day, I had the test to check hormones. Both of these tests were a bit of a rest for me really. I took a CD to the Scan and it was played through my headphones. It was a Yoga Nidra relaxation CD. I also had recorded it onto my MP3 and listened as I sat during the test to check my hydrocortisone levels. The nurse took my blood and injected me with something. She left me for 30 minutes, came back, took more blood, went away for 30 minutes. She came back for more blood, went away then back again etc. You get the picture. I was there for an hour and half, easy peasy. It was not as difficult as I feared, (I got to get some courage like the lion).The relaxation meditation helped, I was very laid back. I would get the result, if I wanted to wait in the waiting room. As this was an endocrine test for hormones the endocrine doctor made an appearance.

"How you doing? Well you look good" he said. I was ready to brag.

"Yes, and look, my legs are getting stronger."

"What you been doing" he continued "whatever it is, keep going"

"I have been swimming." I told him the story of the hydro pool etc.

"Well done" he replied.

The results came back and, hey presto; I was producing enough hydrocortisone for my own needs, no need for the chemicals any more. Yippee! John and I might stop arguing. If I was producing my own hormone, the fight or flight hormone, I would have had too much in my body, therefore couldn't flight so would stay and fight. John and I seemed to not agree on anything and we were both angry at not only my plight but also because he had his own medical problems. He wasn't as robust as he would have liked to care for me. Stefanie and the family were very supportive helping out. Coming in and doing things, cooking, cleaning, washing etc. David and Laura brought in shopping etc. Others kept me company. After the Christmas and New Year holidays, and when everyone had to go back to work, our Liz was at our place almost every day pottering, checking me out. She had been a Ward Sister before she retired so I was in good hands.

The scan results would be at the next appointment in a couple of weeks' time.

For every up there is a down and when the scan results came back it showed some of the tumour was still there. They hadn't got it all out.

"But the surgeon said they got it all". I continued, "very scared now". "Is this a one that couldn't be seen because of the big size of the original tumour?" I asked.

"No, the surgeon must have thought it was safer to get what they could". He looked at me now with fear on my face.

"We will monitor it over time".

It was and still is a benign tumour and very slow growing. The one taken out could have been growing for years. We will do another scan in September see how it is. There is always radiotherapy if it grows".

"No way!" No radiotherapy", I said.

I have seen the results of radiotherapy on brain tumours. Two of my brothers in law had gone this route…they're not with us anymore. So I was worried. It was never good news when we went to hospital appointments. The wicked witch of the North had reared her ugly head again. We went to Costa for a cup of tea.

March is my birthday month. What the hell! We decided to go away to Bowness on Windermere in the Lake District. It is such a beautiful place - lakes, mountains, very scenic, very relaxing and peaceful. I had been here before because, for 3 years we lived in the South Lakeland area near

Carnforth where the old 1930s film "Brief Encounter" was filmed. As it was March it was not very warm, but we tried to do a little walk around which proved easier said than done. As yet my body was not very stable and my balance wasn't good, a: because of the left side of my body and b: because of the eyes. However, we sat by Lake Windermere…until it got too cold, spring in England is cold. We looked in at the specialist shops one-offs in this area, and sat in the hotel having afternoon tea. It was a good little break.

If we didn't go out I would sit and knit. It was suggested to me by Kate, my Newcastle friend. It might help you strengthen your hand and fingers. It wasn't anything wonderful that I knitted. With difficulty I would cast on 50 stitches, knit a border of plain stitches and the rest purl stitches. This was wonderful therapy. I got very cross when I first tried to do it and very sad. In the past I was a knitter, knitting coats, dresses, skirts, Arran jumpers and cardigans for myself, husband and children and anyone who asked, now I had difficulty casting on only 50 stitches. I kept going through blood, sweat, and tears. By the end of that therapy, a good few months later, I had knitted 12 of these squares, and when finished, stitched them all together and called the finished piece a "healing blanket".

Chapter Twenty One

21 "The road to the city of emerald is paved with yellow bricks so you can't miss it"

April 2014

My healing was a slow progression but, by April, we returned the plastic seats which the occupational therapist brought to help me shower over the bath, or to sit at the sink. Both these pieces of equipment were a godsend. At home I still needed, on a daily basis, help with showering, dressing and doing my hair because my left side was improved only in small movements. 'John Frieda'… my John was not, but he dried my hair for a long time because I could not do it myself. Not having the ability to lift my left arm and eventually when I did it was only for a short time, but I kept going to get the messages to my brain on what to do. My hair was dried, but not styled. I kept it shorter than normal. Glad to have found Jason.

May 2014

It was May again. The only good thing to happen in May was Tyler's birthday. The last few Mays were difficult. John's brothers had both died in May.

"I had my eyes tested" said David. He continued "I thought I better get checked out make sure I was ok. The optician said I was fine and a pituitary tumour is not hereditary. He also said it was very rare to have pituitary tumours, so nothing to worry about". "Yes it is rare" I said.

"Only 0.08% of people have them and they are generally benign."[1]

We decided to go to Australia in August. June and July filled our heads with good thoughts. It would be fab to see the Sparks (their married name) and their little sparkler, aged 9 months by then.

June

This was a good month. We spent a week in Scotland, at a place called Moness Country Club, near to Aberfeldy. We loved this place; it was a regular holiday destination over the years, mainly with our David when young. The girls went their own way by this time. We had as good a time as we could. It was lovely because our sister-in-law came and spent a few days with us. We called to see her on our journey. She lives near Edinburgh and worked with a man whose wife had the same condition as me. Anne had invited the lady to meet me. Julie was in her twenties and now had a baby aged 5 months. It seems she had previously had a miscarriage and it was discovered that the reason was the tumour pressing on her pituitary gland. It was good to meet someone else and talk. We had the same condition but different experiences. To remove the tumour she had the traditional surgery - going in through the nose. I laugh at this because in Egyptian times this was how they took out the brain before mummifying a body. So Julie got to be a mummy with a beautiful daughter.

My sister – in - law was amazed by how far I had come in the short time since she saw me at Christmas. By now, with my new swimming skills I had practised in the hydro pool, my arm and leg movement had improved. The test was, could they coordinate and actually do the swimming bit? It was a small leisure pool which I had always been able to swim in. I loved to swim, could swim at the age of 10 and always enjoyed it. I got into the pool very carefully, walking was better but I had to go carefully - didn't want to slip. It was lovely to feel the water on my skin. OK fab, let's go. I lay on the water and began to do the breast stroke which was usually my stroke. It didn't work and I began to go under. I screamed!! It wasn't deep at the shallow end where I was but I had panicked. I was in tears and terrified. I could swim, always had, but now!!! Got out of the pool - I was very upset.

The problem with me is I see everything as a challenge and never give up. I went into the pool every day after that but took along one of those polystyrene long orange snaky things the kids use. I wrapped it around myself and practised the breast stroke until, by the end of the week and holiday, I was able to swim the breast stroke back and forwards across the pool without the snake. I laughed to myself on the last day. A small child with her dad asked if she could use the snake and of course I said yes, thrilled I didn't need it any more.

We did do other things – we went to evening entertainment and a quiz. We did some walking in Aberfeldy. We visited the usual touristy places we always went to when in Scotland: Pitlochry and Stirling. It was a quiet holiday by our standards but better than I could have hoped for in the circumstances.

The down - side of June was my first appointment at the Eye Clinic in the RVI. What a carry on. The appointment was 9.30am and we were there for 3 hours before I saw the Consultant. I had to go through a series of tests to get to how my eyes were working and it took all morning. I knew in my heart of hearts that my eyes were not doing very well since the right eye had opened. I was disappointed at the end of the session when I saw the consultant. She didn't tell me much, and apart from anything else, she didn't have my notes. Through all the tests I got the impression they were focusing on the double vision symptoms I was now showing. The double vision had been there since the right eye had opened. The next appointment was to be in August but we were going to Australia, unfortunately the next appointment was to be December.

July 2014

During this time we met Martin Crosby, a local member of the Pituitary Foundation. The Foundation [1] is supported by families and patients with this condition. John, who could read the information on the website, sent an email to Martin. He responded. It seemed a group of people with pituitary issues met every quarter. They helped to support each other during their challenging time.

I went along to the next meeting at this time and met three others - all with the same condition, but with different experiences. It was very enlightening to hear their stories which can be read on the website - little snippets of how it was for them.

The month ended very excitedly with the arrival of another grandchild this time a girl. David and Laura adopted Phoebe. She was one year old when she arrived in our family. A lovely blonde, blue-eyed girl. She was a cheerful child, smiling a lot and very sociable. We didn't get to spend a great deal of time with her. The rule is that adoptive children have to get used to the new situation with their new mam and dad before they meet other family members. It all worked well because we were going to Australia for a month and would not have the chance to see her anyway.

Chapter Twenty Two

22 "Somewhere Over the Rainbow"

August 2014

"Baby Bude has grown up since we got here three weeks ago" said John.

"Yes, it's amazing how quickly babies grow and develop" I continued "it's great he's trying to crawl so we didn't miss a first". I was able now to pick Bude up and carry him for a short while. Mainly, I was able to get down on the floor and play with him and feed him at meal times. We even babysat one night while Claire and Tony went to a restaurant around the corner for a meal. He was as good as gold and never woke up until they put their key in the door.

"It's been a great time being with them all and lovely to be of help while Claire and Tony packed their possessions in boxes ready to move house", I said.

We looked after Bude while they did this. We took him out in his pram. We looked after him. Walking, pushing the pram, and baby to parks, to see the ducks and other animals. Not just ordinary parks. One was "Albert Park" where the Australian Grand Prix is held (also lakes and play areas there). Going to little activities in the library and other places in South Melbourne where they lived. Melbourne is a great looking city with old tall colonial houses. There is an "Emerald Hill" and even "The Yellow Brick Road" insurance company. Melbourne and the family is a good place to heal my heart.

"Yes it has been very good" I said.

"We are stronger because of all the things we've been doing" replied John. He continued, "Yes, but sad we are going back home next week".

It had been a busy time here in Australia. We did a lot. We were able to go for lunch on a "Restaurant Tram" going around Melbourne. It had been booked for our wedding anniversary in November 2013 and postponed till this month. Great - food was good and service fab. We met other Australians while eating and sightseeing and thoroughly enjoyed the experience.

We were also lucky enough to spend a night in the best hotel in Melbourne; courtesy of Donna, a good friend of Claire's who said

"Care package - it's for you to help with your recovery Kath, enjoy!"

I felt like Pretty Woman and couldn't stop grinning. The room was on the 45th floor and there were stunning views both during the day and in the evening. Our room also overlooked Melbourne Cricket Ground. This was a place John got to visit the last time we were in Australia. This treat was for John after his illness, also a care package courtesy of Donna.

Claire and Tony organised a weekend to a town called Ballarat. This town was where gold was discovered in 1854. This was an ancestral trail for me because my ancestors came here and struck gold and making their home in Australia in the 1850s.

My ancestors landed in southern Australia near Melbourne. It seems those emigrants who were entrepreneurs, settled here and as we all know, the convicts were deported from England to Sydney, Australia.

The best part of the month was of course being with baby Bude and Claire and Tony. It was somewhat like the scarecrow and the lion going along the yellow brick road to see the Wizard of Oz. They were seeking a heart (Tin Man) and courage (Lion), with Dorothy trying to get home (back to good health). There were a lot of challenges for me along this yellow brick road. Flying 12,000 miles to Australia was not without the challenge of the flight (another story); scaling the stairs in Claire and Tony's three floor town house; going out and about in a town where I did not already have a map in my head. It all took a lot of courage.

I had become bitter about what had happened to my and John's health. Why me, why us, what had we done to deserve all this ill health? The bitterness evaporated somewhat coming to Australia. Seeing and being with the baby. Children are our joy, if we let them be. Spending time with Claire and Tony, who are inspirational people, coming to live on the other side of the world, was such a tonic.

As I said above, Claire is a yoga teacher and we went along each week to classes. The theme of each session was … the heart… All this love was helping me feel a lot better.

"Let's have a look at your Kindle" said Tony one evening.

He realised I was having great difficulties reading the books on it as well as looking at my emails. I would get upset and frustrated with it all.

"I am working with Vision Australia the equivalent of our Royal National Institute for the Blind (RNIB) in UK"

Tony worked for a solution partner of Microsoft in Australia. He was up to date with IT and Software.

"Here it is - the narrator" he said.

A voice sounded as Tony touched the screen.

The voice would say what was on the screen and which button to press depending on what action was needed. The narrator that Tony had found was in settings called Accessibility. The Kindle could be made more user-friendly for those with learning difficulties or any kind of disability. Liberation! I remembered this facility was also on computers. When I was teaching in college 14 to 19 year olds and adults with learning difficulties, one of students were visually impaired, therefore I would adapt his PC to make on screen text and icons easier to see. Just like the scarecrow, I already had a brain. Just like me always searching for something I already had.

September 2014

Looking back to the beginning of the year, I could see how far I had come. My first trip out after the operation was for a weekend in February 2014 to Nottingham - a Scrabble Tournament, which John had organised. I joined the scrabble crowd once a month for all of 2014. If I was unable to go along, it would have been necessary for John to organise help for me each weekend he was away. If we couldn't get help then John would not have been able to go and leave me. Therefore, we agreed to rise to the challenge of going away.

We always went by car to each event, Nottingham, Harrogate, Morecambe, Birmingham, Reading or Southsea. It was great ....being away ..... Sitting on my settee at home to sitting on a settee in Hotels. Food cooked, room tidied up and bedding and towels changed regularly. Also, these weekends were respite for John from being on call 24/7.

In Nottingham in February, my friend from Lincoln came to stay in the hotel with us. It was lovely because I hadn't seen her since the operation. We never shut up. In Birmingham, my niece came to see us at that hotel and we went to her house for coffee. She was also an ophthalmic person and she tested my eyes and recommended glasses for me. Another niece came to our hotel in Southsea and we went to the local park with her and two of my great nephews aged 2 and 1 year old. It was great fun and so, for all of 2014 I went away each month, which helped me to see my progress as the year wore on. There were difficult times, even cutting up my food with other people at the table. "You're doing really well" said a person sitting next to me. "My Jack couldn't cut up his food after he had had a stroke". I was stunned. I was hoping I wasn't being watched, but alas I was. It was difficult to find my own way around each hotel but I managed and of course I was unable to play scrabble which I had done before. Also in the past, I helped out doing what was called "running". In scrabble, two players play but, if a word is placed on the board, the opponent can challenge the word if they are not sure it is a proper word. The person would write the challenged word on the challenge paper and, as the runner, I would collect the paper take it to the director and the word would be checked for its validity. I would take the paper, back to the players. I couldn't do this anymore. Such a lot of things I had lost.

However, one such scrabble weekend was particularly memorable - that was in Anglesey.....This was the first time I had shopped totally on my own in the past 6 months. I needed a travel spoon, fork and knife, plastic things. I walked to a mariner's shop in the port, about 20 metres – a long way for me on my own without hanging onto John. I had a little look around the shop and, as I couldn't see what I wanted, asked "hello, do you have any plastic cutlery please?"

"Yes of course" replied the women behind the counter. "We have these things" she showed me. "It's a spoon, fork and knife in one". "That's just what I am looking for" I responded. Smiling inside I handed over the money and left the shop. I followed a route around a few stationary cars to get back to our car.

"Well done" John shouted thrilled that I had not only got back to the car all in one piece but also that I had gone into a shop and bought something for the first time since the operation. Yes, it was tricky walking on my own but also talking and asking for something …basically interaction and handing over money and getting back to the car. A simple thing to do for those able-bodied people but for me it was like climbing up Snowdonia. Hooray, hooray an achievement!

I must have been feeling a lot better because I didn't want to go to the Scrabbles in October and November. My friend in Lincoln said "Come and stay with me. You will be company for me. I am not driving because I am going to have my cataracts removed but you know us, we will talk each other to death. It sounded fun. John took me but we were hardly in the house five minutes when my friend's son-in-law rang to say his wife, my friend's daughter, Gemma, was in hospital with suspected appendicitis. I was company for my friend because we went back and forwards to the hospital that weekend as Gemma had to have an operation. It was amazing what I could do when I didn't think about what my problems were.

In November I stayed with my sister. We also had an enjoyable weekend but not our usual sort of weekend. Sis is a walker and I was before all this stuff, but not being able to do the usual activities made me feel disabled. Sis could see I was a bit low. We had words and she said "You are bitter and twisted now our Kath, and I think you need help". She was right. Having the operation and my situation had pushed all of my "I am the victim" buttons.

Chapter Twenty Three

23 "Dorothy built a splendid fire that warmed her and made her feel less lonely"

November 5 2014

It was our wedding anniversary. "Are you enjoying yourself?" said John as we ate our afternoon tea. We were sitting in Baltic restaurant overlooking the river, and the bridges. The Baltic was a building which housed contemporary art. It is on the banks of the River Tyne in Newcastle upon Tyne, UK. We had decided that this anniversary would be more joyful than the 2013 one. We'd been out all day. In our marriage we loved to travel, stay in hotels and frequent coffee shops. We wanted this day to be a celebration, not only of our anniversary, but also a celebration of the things we loved doing together.

Our day began travelling by car to the local garden centre for brunch. We took the bus into the city of Newcastle.

"Can you take our photograph, please?" I asked a passer-by outside of the Civic Centre "We were married here 43 years ago and want to have a picture" I said excitedly. She was willing to oblige.

It was coffee time and we went into the local Costa coffee. This was where Newcastle University students frequented. We reminisced about our student years... at the grand young age of 40-ish onwards.

We walked down Northumberland Street looking in the shop windows. Then it was afternoon tea, here at the Baltic.

We had booked a room at one of the quayside hotels "Mal Maison" which means "Bad House" - always wanted to be bad girl on the Quayside, in my youth, when the sailors came ashore!! Now here I was!!

We booked a good room with good views to watch the bonfire night celebrations, which was just great. There were fireworks crackling and banging. There was a brightly lit rockets speeding up towards the dark sky. There are five bridges over the River Tyne. On this night and others in the winter the bridges are well lit. There are also lights from the buildings, giving a magical feeling to the river. The whole day was such fun and gave us great joy and hope for the future.

Chapter Twenty Four

24 "It was a very wide ditch, and when they crept up to the edge and
looked into it they could see it was very deep"

It was 16 November and I rang my Lincoln friend to wish her happy
birthday.

"Thank you" she said.

"How you doing?" she asked.

"How long is it now since your operation?"

"A year on 26 November" I replied.

We continued with the chit-chat but something inside had stirred. When the
call ended I felt so sad. I realised it was about a year since the operation. I had
been so involved in getting well I hadn't noticed the passing of time. Now I
felt dreadful. I was still not well. Yes I could walk. My mobility had greatly
improved, but still a way to go. My right eye was open, but it didn't work
properly, there was still double vision. I was so pleased when the eye opened.
Each morning as I awoke and slowly opened easily my left eye, the right eye
even slower I looked up at the central light hanging from the ceiling. Looking
each morning at the light became my barometer on the progress off my right
eye. In the beginning, I thought the double vision would go away as my eye
and brain function improved.

I had just been to the eye clinic in the RVI. The eye tests showed things were
still the same. There was loss of peripheral vision in both eyes. The right eye
muscle didn't move well. They were not sure if my right eye was not working
properly because of the bleed, trauma during the operation or weakness to
the nerves going from the eye to the brain and back again. It seems both of
our eyes see images differently. When the images from each eye go to the

brain, the two visions are sent back to the eyes as a single vision and all is fine. That wasn't working for me. The ophthalmic consultant suggested I have a certificate of visual impairment "There is a lot of help out there and it might help you".

Also there was still a residual tumour in my head and the doctor wanted me to have radiotherapy, which I resisted.

"Let's get you well and you might consider it" he said.

I sat and cried. All my efforts at getting back to full strength and ability had not fully worked. I couldn't go out alone, wasn't able to walk around unaided because my balance was affected. My car was sitting there not being used. My independence and freedom had gone. Without John I was housebound.

John and I seemed to be arguing again.

"You're so angry" he said.

"It's you who is angry about it all, not me" I would retort.

I blamed him for having been ill himself two years previous and me having to take care of him.... It went on and on. I made the decision that I wanted Psychiatric help. The Doctor offered it to me after the operation. He said it might help me come to terms with my new situation. I didn't feel I needed it then. Now I did. At my next Endocrine appointment it was agreed that I could speak to someone. The doctor would sort it for me.

Christmas came again as it always does. I put on a brave face and we moved on to 2015, another year had passed. What did the future hold for me and us? I wasn't a young person - 67 years old and at this point my future was very bleak.

Part Three

"The Emerald City"

Chapter Twenty Five

25 "I am OZ, the Great and Terrible. Who are you?"

"Mam don't make New Year resolutions, we never keep them anyway" said Stefanie. She continued "This year I am going to think about counting my blessings".

"What's that about?" I asked.

Stefanie handed me a piece of paper. On it were words. These words were headings.

"Think about and write down things you are grateful for".

"Write your blessings under each heading "When you're done count your blessings".

"What have I got to be grateful for?" I retorted.

"Just do it Mam" she said.

After she went home I looked again at the paper. Ok I thought, let's give it a try. I got out my writing stuff and set to. Here is what came up.

Surprise Gifts	Accomplished goals	Lots of Love Moments	Daily Blessings	The beauty of Nature
Ruby Slippers	Getting well	Having family around this past year	Waking up every day	Seeing a deer
Visitors from Australia	Walking again	A new Grand-daughter	Looking forward in good days	Watching the seasons change
New Precious Grand daughter	Walking unaided	Sharing Special Bude moments	Ability to move arms and legs	Seeing snow drops
Xmas Jumper	Right Eye Opened	Tyler saying "grandma you can do stairs properly now"	Feeling physically stronger	Spring daffodils and Tulips
Soup Maker	Got to Australia		Enjoying and being with others	Trees blossoming in the spring

There was a lot to be grateful for. I had come a long way. So to quote Louise L Hay, All is well.

I still had hope. I decided 2015 was to be my rehabilitation year. I did the recovery thing in 2014. Let's get out there and live my life to the full, not just a half of life.

Chapter Twenty Six

26 "Can you give me a brain?" asked the Scarecrow"

February 2015

In February I began having counselling. I saw a psychologist once a fortnight. At the same time she recommended I should attend wellbeing sessions run by the psychology department. These sessions were also once a fortnight. After each session I could discuss any issues with the psychologist. They were Tuesday afternoons in the Royal Victoria Infirmary. John would take me. There was never a car parking space in the hospital car park. We would take the car to the "park and ride" at Stefanie's house. Then take the bus to the hospital. We were always too early for the sessions. We would have lunch in the hospital restaurant....not fine dining... but it seemed fun. These sessions seemed to make us more cheerful. They were open to anyone and John had to take me to them, so he stayed and took part. They seemed to be helpful to him after his health traumas. We attended the sessions for 10 weeks until May.

Session 1 was all about Stress Management and relaxation. When we are stressed our bodies produce hormones which change our body chemistry making it go into fight or flight mode. Modern day examples of this are: when we are ill; when the boss shouts at us and we feel threatened. We all know our stressors. Our breathing changes. Our heart beats faster. Other organs respond. Our digestive system closes down. We need to be ready to fight, Flight, even freeze if we see a tiger. It all goes back to our reptilian brain. This state isn't appropriate in modern times, but our bodies haven't adapted yet. However, it is a safety mechanism to protect us against any kind of threat.

We were shown how to use breathing and mindfulness techniques. Using these techniques calms us, brings us back to the now. We stop projecting our fear thoughts into the future. Worrying about something happening that never will. Also, churning over and over the past, nothing can be changed. When the past is over it is over. No point in using energy and getting stressed. By practising relaxation and mindfulness we become more peaceful.

Session 2 was about managing worrying and uncertainty. How these anxieties can lead to stress which impacts on our physical health. We learnt how to let go of some of our thoughts which were not fact but us projecting a future situation that was not likely to happen. We also learnt, what to do to stop it all.

Session 3 was low moods and how to adapt to a health condition. This was about negative thoughts, loss of confidence, feeling lonely, feeling a sense of loss and much more. Identifying what triggers them and how to identify and avoid the triggers.

Session 4 was about managing activities and how to pace then. How to look at all the activities a person does and adapt them to fit the new situation. Take time doing things and give oneself plenty of time to do things.

Session 5   This was about managing thoughts and thinking. It was about identifying what we were thinking about and, if negative, changing thoughts to a positive.

One of these sessions made me realise I had been grieving for what had happened and what I had lost and accepting the new situation.

Doing these modalities together gave me back my normality and my life. Things changed because I had changed.

Chapter Twenty Severn

27 "Can you give me a Heart?" asked the Tin Man"

February 2015

Into my life, at this time, came a way to heal my broken heart. It was broken not only because I never got to Australia in 2013 for the birth of my second grandson, but also because of my condition and what I had been through. At the end of February Claire sent me an email with a link.

"Have a look at this, you will be very interested" she wrote.

The email link was to the Seventh Tapping World Summit 2015. This summit was an internet based summit about tapping. It was online for 10 days and each day I could sign in and listen to not only interviews with scientists, doctors, psychologists and tapping practitioners talking about tapping, what it is and its benefits. Also there were audio meditations which I could tap along to in relation to health, trauma, the past, weight loss, and much, much more.

This, my new healing modalities proper title is "Emotional Freedom Techniques" (EFT), known as Tapping. It is used a lot in psychology in USA. This modality is a combination of psychology and ancient Chinese meridian tapping, which is light touching with the finger tips. Tapping is also about calming the fight or flight response in the Amygdala to bring about a feeling of being safe. The gremlins are not real.

I tapped along every day, using positive statements to bring about change, in a big way. It was great. It helped me to release all sorts of emotions of sadness, anger, resentment, bitterness etc. The Chinese believe that emotions or energy gets stuck in the body and it might be this that causes illness. There was a lot, both since the surgery, even from the past. Therefore, from the beginning of March until way into July I tapped on a regular daily basis. I felt so much better. My mood changed, my broken heart began to mend. I felt that I was slowly returning to normal.

I also discovered…Dru Yoga … online. In 2014 I went along to a few yoga classes in a healing centre. The sessions lasted about one and a half hours. I felt the sessions were too long for me. I sometimes could not attend for reasons of illness. John would drive me to the sessions and sometimes my friend Liz would give me a lift home. There were times John might not be well, or just couldn't make it. No independence and paying up front for 5 or 6 sessions meant when I did not attend I didn't get my money refunded. That's just the way it is. I realised I could not commit to anything. When I found Yoga on line and with two months free trial I was so very pleased. I now pay £9.99 a month. I have benefitted from doing Yoga and do sessions 2 or 3 times a week. It is good value for money as there are also relaxations and meditation sessions and more. I did this yoga whenever I wanted and at home, no getting lifts to Yoga classes now. I took my time and did short sessions of 10 minutes to help build strength and stamina. As I got stronger I extended the sessions: such joy. I have enjoyed yoga for about 15-20 years and now I can do it at my own pace again. By August I was doing 1 hour sessions. My co-ordination isn't to full strength but I do what I can.

"Meet yourself where you are today". Claire would say.

I keep going, going and going, it's fun.

Chapter Twenty Eight

28 "Can you give me some courage?" the lion asked the Wizard"

March 2015

I was invited to the Low Sight Unit at Sight Service within Bensham Hospital. I was eligible now because I had a certificate of Partial sighted/visually impaired - another Wizard that changed my life. The service provides support to those people who have sight problems or are blind. I was referred there after I was certified vision impaired. I began to have a glimpse of hope that my life could be better. The optician there showed me how I could use the sight I did have to my advantage. If I look out of the corner of my eye a certain way I can see clearly. What a revelation, all was not lost. To top it all a lady (Dawn) sitting in the room taking notes said she understood what I was saying about my sight. When she was 15 Dawn had a brain tumour removed. It left her with poor vision. She has lived her life, worked, married and had a child who is now grown up… such an inspiration. Dawn trained for two years to become a rehabilitation officer and she is such an inspiration and I call her "my Dawn of a new era". She takes me out and about and encourages me and others with eye sight problems to become confident and get back their independence.

On the 31st of March I had a fab afternoon. I went down to the Metrocentre on the train with my new best friends Dawn and Holly from Sight Service. They have encouraged me to regain my confidence and independence, as well as courage…..just like the lion in Oz. Dawn took me around on public transport. This helped me to regain my confidence being out and about. Her PA Holly also goes with us, our clear eyes. The train journey from my home in Wylam was easy for me, just one stop. I had the map etc. in my head anyway because I used this train to take me into the city centre of Newcastle before my operation. Getting on and off the train wasn't as daunting as I thought it would be, I never went to Metrocentre on the train - so it was an adventure. When we got off the train it was a short walk to the lift to take us into the centre. There are stairs, but the lift was best at this time in my life. Dawn explained the push button system in the lift designed for visually impaired or blind people. Then hey presto we were at the correct floor, which took us into the centre. I was using my symbol white stick - never did that before. It wasn't too bad. The stick was easy to carry. I couldn't see if people were looking or not. We went into Weatherspoon's, an eatery and pub, for a coffee and food. A cup of coffee, only £1 in here, so definitely will come back and with hubby. We talked about all sorts including, "You Can Heal Your Life" book written by Louise L Hay and the power of positive thinking. We had a little walk around the Blue and Green malls and up the biggest escalator, with a few tips on safety and sensibility when using it. Didn't do the down escalator - wasn't keen before, so even less keen now. Hey, never say never, who knows what will happen when I get more confidence? We went for the 3.30p.m. train back to Wylam as instructed by the ticket collector on the train from Wylam.

Managed to get on to the train ok – "mind the gap". This was a posh train, very clean and new-looking, going to Carlisle via Wylam, usually not so modern. Ticket collector came …"tickets from Metrocentre". ..Handed them over… he looked…

"Sorry this is the express train. It's not stopping in Wylam, first stop Prudhoe" he said.

Did I panic? No I didn't. I was with the girls and it was fun. The collector made a note on my ticket explaining things and we could get off at Prudhoe and get the train back to Wylam. After all, we were told by the ticket collector on the train from Wylam to Metrocentre that we could get the 3.02 pm, or the 3.30 pm back, before the 4pm rush hour or our tickets would not be valid after 4pm. Glad to have got over that one easily. I was with company and it won't be a problem for me if it happens again, been there done that. I will check the timetable properly in future. Never mind - the adventure was good. Home in one piece, great time - will do that again.

It was March, my birthday having been on 28th. I was 68 years of age, and still do not know what I wanted to be when I grew up.

April 2015

On April 9 I did my homework. I decided today was to be the perfect day to challenge myself by going out. I did my envisioning meditation. I visualised my journey out and about. During this I said to myself….

"Whether you think you can, or you think you cannot then you are right" (Henry Ford)

I was ready…..

To begin my adventure I had to get to the train station. As said above I have done this often when fully sighted. Now it was all down to me. I successfully got through the woods from my apartment. It's a lovely walk. I live in a gated place, so next step out of the gates. There is a number key pad used through a code to open the gate. After a few tries the gate opened. Next challenge, walk down the three flights of stairs, 30 stairs in all, onto the station platform. The train to the Metrocentre left from the other side of the track. I crossed the train track. Lucky for me the barrier didn't go down, indicating a train was coming. There is a stairway over the track to the other side. Not for me these days. Phew! Phew! The train was on time. Got onto it, avoiding the gap between the train and track. People must have thought I was mad. I couldn't stop smiling. I made it.

"Return ticket to the Metrocentre?" I asked the conductor.

I had my money ready, didn't want to rummage around in my purse.

"What time will you return?" he asked.

"Don't know" I replied, "Why?"

"This is a limited ticket only until 4 o'clock. No travelling after 4 with this ticket".

I had a senior rail card and could not use the ticket after 4. Never mind, it was only 11a.m. and knew I would be back well before the Cinderella deadline of 4pm. The train pulled out of the station. The journey was short, almost ten minutes. I was nervous getting off. That gap... I used the lift to take me up to the walk way into the centre. I then had to use a lift to take me onto the ground floor. I was so pleased with myself. I was still smiling. Walked past a café, decided to try my new skills and go in and have lunch on my own. It was such a long time since I had been to the shopping centre. This was a new place called "Spuds You Like" I was so very nervous. It was the first time in more than a year I was out on my own. I couldn't see the menu properly but hey, it was spuds, I couldn't go wrong. I would have eaten Sh** with Sugar, I was out on my own. Independence here I come, limitations gone.

Had a bit wander, not too far? In fact I realised how far the walk was between each mall. I looked at a couple of summer tops in British Home Stores (BHS).They didn't have my size. There might have been my size. I was too proud to ask for assistance. I will look on internet...shop on-line, but got the idea of what I would like for a summer top by being in the shop. I did bump into the wall within the shop. I laughed when I did this. It was my own fault; too busy talking to a woman, not looking where I was going. By the end of the trip out I was worn out. It took all of my strength and will power to get back to the train station. As I was standing on the platform awaiting the train, which was delayed, I laughed to myself. There were a couple of announcements.

"The 3.02 is delayed by 7 minutes".

The next announcement said delayed by 6 minutes. Then back to 7 minutes late. We on the platform laughed and it was so good to be out. I thought to myself "I am free, I am free". Train arrived, got on, remembering to mind the gap between the train and platform. Home now, so proud but so very tired.

Three hours in all of independence and freedom. Yippee, Yippee, perfect day. So proud of myself. Going out on my own for the first time in 18 months. Thank you Dawn for giving me the confidence to do it. Tonight off to another meditation class and who knows what my next homework will be.

During this month I began to attend a 7 week course delivered by Sight Service called "My Sight My Future". It has been very informative and also very confidence building. There have been 7 regular people every week, all with different eye and other problems and meeting each one gave me a "what have I got to complain about?" One of the ladies is 92 and with eye problems and still getting around; another lady comes and brings her guide dog that lies on the floor under the table - wouldn't know she was there.

We got shown different technologies to help e.g. talking books, magnifiers and one which I bought that plugs into the telly. It looks like a computer mouse and by moving it across a page of any kind, the words and images are magnified onto the TV screen.

Another session was about looking after oneself when out and about. For example how to cross the road safely, use the crossing and identify things by using our senses e.g. smells sound etc. to know where we might be.

Following the course in June I had to take courage and walk into our local village. We live about half mile outside of Wylam. The walk involved descending the three flights of stairs, walking over the level crossing and walking about ¾ mile or more to our doctors to collect a prescription for John as he wasn't too well. I had to go and get it dispensed at the pharmacy. I also crossed the road to buy bread at the local small shop. Then the reverse walks back the route I came along, to get home. It would have been about two miles there and back. So well done, well done me. Thank you, thank you, to the rehabilitation staff for their help and advice and to the service being available for people like me.

Chapter Twenty Nine

29 "Life goes on"

During all of this, life still goes on. We still Skype to keep up to date with Bude's development and I was so very pleased one day when Bude appeared

"Mwah, mwah, mwah, Grandma" my now 17 month old Australian grandson said. These sounds were in fact kisses, and he said them as he came up close to the webcam. We would Skype something each week to keep in touch. It was a fab technology. We could all see each other, as much as if they were here in England so the distance of 12,000 miles didn't seem so wide. Even if we never got to Australia for his birth, we had watched Bude grow and develop. We didn't miss any stage of his development. His first smile, first tooth, first steps and his first words. Theses treasured moments came to us either on Skype or little video clips. Claire would take and send them to Grandpa and Grandma. We could play them over and over again.

The voice of Tony interrupted our chat.

"Come on Bude, bath time and bed".

"Mwah, mwah" Bude said again.

"Night, night Bude" I said.

"Night! Night! Grandma" he replied.

Tony took him to the bath.

"Ah Mam that's the first time he's said night, night. With me and Tony he will reply "bye bye" when we say night, night, to him.

"That's fab Claire, we heard another first, thank you".

Bude was very vocal now and interacted with his Grandpa and Grandma on Skype. Of course in the beginning he was hours old but we could see him. We watched him playing in the garden, climbing over the furniture, playing with toys, I got him a book with the sounds of trains, fire engines, dumper trucks etc. and when reading the book to him and pressing the buttons to make the sounds he went away and came back with his dumper truck to show us......fab, he could play with granny ......but the thing missing is the cuddles and touching.....he thought we lived in the television or the I Pad or laptop or even in the photographs on the wall. We so missed them all but hey life goes on and our grandson in Australia proved that I had come a long way in the past 17 months on my healing journey.

Life goes on and April 10 was my granddaughter, Phoebe's 2nd birthday. Phoebe and my other grandchild Tyler came along with other cousins and enjoyed her party at soft play. What an eventful year. Phoebe has brought laughter, joy and courage to the family. I am so grateful I am still here to hear her laughter, her early words. Also, I am able to see her even if it is tricky.

Tyler the now eldest grandchild at 7 years old is growing into a sensible boy, doing very well in school but still cannot understand why granny cannot drive. One day he said "grandma you look perfect to drive now, can we go out?

"Ah pet, we used to have such fun in the car. Thank you Tyler, I must be looking ok now" I continued.

" Yes, I still have driving skills, but my eyes do not see properly and that is why I cannot drive the car, but we can still have fun, what shall we do?" I asked.

Chapter Thirty

30 "It's all in your own backyard"

I visited the hospital at my usual 6 monthly appointment to see the Doctor to get the scan results.

"The residual of tumour looks stable…. we will continue to monitor on a 6 month basis" said the endocrine doctor.

I feel I have come to the end of the yellow brick road. The journey has shown me, like the lion in the wizard I have courage and we all have it.

I have a brain. I can read and write ….I kept a diary and I am writing this story. No need to go searching for one like the scarecrow. Also, to quote someone, not sure who... I think, therefore I am. Seeing the psychologist helped me realise my brain was just tired after what it had been through. It was also pointed out I was grieving for the things I had lost.

My heart was there all the time. It was just so very, very sad. The tapping helped me disperse the bitterness and other emotions to find my loving heart underneath it all again.

The last Wizard to help me came in the form of my writing. It was my cousin Peter who instigated this new phase in my writing life. During the month of May I was invited and went along to Peter's book launch. He is a local history writer and he had finished a book called "Clubs of Gateshead" - Gateshead is where we lived as children. His publisher introduced the launch and chatted about Gateshead's history. He asked the audience what they could remember about the town.

"If anyone has memories come and talk to me".

Well I did, and to cut a long story short I am now writing a local history book entitled "Memories of Gateshead" It's about my childhood in the 1950s. Every cloud has a silver lining.

Also during this May month, I attended a workshop called "I am the Author." I wanted to learn skills on how to write my life story. I and others at the workshop were lucky enough to read out on a radio program, called "Spice FM", a piece we had written during the session. The radio program was also videoed. It is on YouTube. The video is called "I am the Author". So, not only am I viral, but the title might be a self-fulfilling prophecy. How about that then? Watch this space. My future is bright.

Chapter Thirty One

31 "Oh, Aunt Em I am so glad to be home again"

July 2015

It's the end of July and, confidence abounds, I am walking out and about on my own comfortably. John has been unwell, admitted in hospital and I coped admirably with it all.

In October it will be Pituitary Awareness month nationally. I have sent a small account to the Pituitary Foundation of my pituitary experience. They are going to put it onto their website. A piece might go into the "Pituitary Life" magazine in the spring.

I am now a volunteer with Sight Services. I need, and want to help out in some way. I am a digital buddy supporting individuals in their learning of how to use IPads, tablets, Kindles. There is also software for the blind and sight impaired which I am learning to be in a position to pass the knowledge onto others. I was an Information Technology Teacher before I retired. I will also help people with their mobile phones and other digital equipment produced for those with sight problems.

I help out each month at the local Northumbria Healing Centre. The public can drop in and receive energy healing.

In November, I am going to train to become a Tapping practitioner. Busy, busy, what with all this stuff and writing a local history book, doing the research. Now and again, John and I look after our grandchildren. There is a lot going on all the time. Just living, where it will go, who knows. Life goes on and on without us doing anything to help it. Hopefully we will go to Australia again, in the not too distant future.

It's all still there, tricky eyes. I had an eye clinic appointment in August. I was discharged. The consultant decided no need for me to go back, my eyes were stable and I could attend my general optician - if any problems I could see the GP and I could be referred again. I am pleased about this, on the one hand, but sad on the other. There is nothing more they can do at this stage. I have been invited by Durham University to take part in a pilot training computer based exercise. I will hopefully train my brain to compensate for my field vision loss. My brain and eyes, maybe, can learn a different way of seeing things. It's a six month program called DREX that means Durham Reading and Exploration. So who knows where that will take me?

The residual tumour is still there, I think. I have another scan in Nov/Dec. My left side is still a bit weak but life goes on. And I will keep going as long as I am able. What else can I do?? I cannot believe I have gone through major surgery and survived. I know the past is gone - maybe like Dorothy it was all a dream. What the future holds no-one knows. Therefore, the only place to live is in the present moment, the now.

All is well.

Everything is working out

For my highest good

Out of this situation only good will come.

I am safe.

Epilogue

It has been a long journey along the yellow brick road to the Emerald City of wellness. I have grown and learnt a lot about myself. I have been lucky to have wizards to help me.

I realised that there was no need to search outside of myself for answers. All the answers to all the questions are inside of me.

Like Dorothy and the Scarecrow, Lion and Tin Man I found that "everything is in your own backyard". Within us are courage, strength, and a brain. We have the intelligence to take control of our own healing and life. We have a heart, filled with compassion, kindness and love for ourselves and others around us.   Family and friends who help us - we can heal ourselves and begin to live life again. We get to click our ruby slippers together and repeat:

"There is no place like home"

Notes

Chapter 7

1 The Healing Codes
It seems that we give out the most energy from our finger tips. If the fingers
are pointed at different places on the face for a period of time (6 minutes) at a
time, the process can change the energy centres in the body.

2 Tapping
This looks strange if you watch someone doing it. There are energy points on
different parts of the face: on the inside corners of the eyebrows; on the
outsides of the eyes; under the eye, under the nose, and under the chin. Also
points on the collarbone and under the arm. Using the finger tips I could
gently tap on these points in a sequence.

3 Alternative Nose Breathing
I did this by breathing through alternative nostrils. This can be done while
closing the other nostril with either thumb or finger. This practice can clear
the mind and bring about relaxation.

4 Yoga Mudras
Mudras are hand gestures e.g. placing the thumb and finger tips together, the
thumb and each of the other finger tips together. Each action was difficult for
the left hand to do. I used the right hand to place the thumb and finger in the
correct position. I knew that each finger gesture helped a different part of my
lungs to breathe helping my breathing to improve.

5 Yoga Nidra – The Blissful Relaxation
Most people sleep without resolving their tensions.
Yoga Nidra is relaxing each individual part of the body. The mind
concentrates on a particular part which means the mind is not thinking about
upsetting thoughts.

Yoga Nidra means sleep after throwing of the burdens,
It is the experience of total relaxation." Swami Saraswati

6 Positive Affirmations
This modality is about changing our negative thoughts into positive thoughts. The writer Louise Hay and others believe we create our life by the thoughts we think and the words we speak.

7 Physical exercises

Stomach crunches while lying down in bed. This was me trying to lift my body off the bed, even if half of my body could not move.

Chapter 18

1 Energy Healing

"Healing has been practiced around the world for thousands of years and is linked to both eastern and western traditions. In our western context, healing is usually delivered by a light touch on the body (fully clothed), or by placing hands just above the body. Healing can also be offered by distant healing, where the healer and the client are in different locations

2 Shiatsu

"Shiatsu is a form of therapeutic bodywork from Japan. It uses kneading, pressing, soothing, tapping, and stretching techniques and is performed without oils through light, comfortable clothing".

3 Tapping

"Emotional Freedom Technique (EFT) a type of Meridian Tapping that combines ancient Chinese acupressure and modern psychology with startling results. From pain relief, to healing childhood traumas, to clearing limiting financial beliefs, to weight loss, body image and food cravings, to fears and phobias, Tapping is proving to be a powerful, well-researched and easy to learn and apply technique. Tapping utilizes the body's energy meridian points by stimulating them with your fingertips – literally tapping into your body's own energy and healing power"

4 The Healing Codes

"Numerous health experts say that the number one killer on the planet is stress. Most physical and nonphysical health problems have long-term, physiological stress as their origin. The Healing Codes activate powerful healing centers that can allow the body to heal itself of almost anything. They do this by removing the stress from the body, thus allowing the neuro-immune system to take over its job of healing whatever is wrong in the body.

5 Ayurvedic Healing

Ayurvedic medicine also known as Ayurveda -- is one of the world's oldest holistic (whole-body) healing systems. It was developed thousands of years ago in India. It is based on the belief that health and wellness depend on a delicate balance between the minds, body, and spirit.

Resources

www.druyogaonline.com

www.hayhouse.com

www.northumbriahealers.co.uk

www.takingcharge.csh.edu

www.thetappingsolution.com

www.thehealingcodes.com

www.theayurvedicclinic.com

http://glynisrose.com/

https://www.pituitary.org.uk

About the Author

I am Kathleen Harrison, currently a volunteer Trustee with a local charity "Sight Service" in the North East of England U.K. We provide a service to those who are blind or partially sighted. I am married to John and I have two daughters, a son, and four grandchildren.

My first published book is "Memories of Gateshead" . It is a non-fiction local history book, set in Gateshead, Tyne and Wear, U.K.. The story is about my family , the area in which I lived, and Society in the 1950s.

Qualifications

Before I retired I taught Information Communications Technology to youngsters from the age of 14-19. As well as this I taught young at heart adults up to the age of 80 years.

My qualifications are;

- Batchelor of Science First Class Honours Degree in Information Communications Technology.

- Batchelor of Arts in Social Science Second Class degree

Printed in Great Britain
by Amazon